"In her new book Get Noticed . . . Get Referrals, Jill Lublin has given us a simple-to-follow, step-by-step blueprint for cutting through the chatter and really focusing attention on that all-important message about our business and ourselves. She has an uncanny way of taking a complicated subject and making it easy for us to execute. Once again, Jill has proven that she is the 'queen of getting noticed' by weaving together business networking with the key elements of PR and publicity, while injecting us with key success principles in the process."

—**Jeffrey Howard**, "The MasterMind Mentor," International speaker, author, entrepreneur, and business coach/ mentor (www.MasterMindMentor.com).

"Ready, aim, fire. Jill Lublin has hit the mark with this one. If you want to learn how to promote your business or yourself, follow this format and you won't miss your target."

—**Elaine Allison**, Author, *The Velvet Hammer, PowHERful Leadership Lessons for Women Who Don't Golf*

"Jill Lublin has a gift and is considered to be the Queen of Networking. Through this book she will teach you how to 'Get Noticed.' Jill is the connector in any room and her book is certain to show you just how to perfect your approach. Ready, set, enter and be ready to 'Get Noticed.' "

—**Melissa Prandi**, MPM, author of *The Unofficial Guide to Managing Rental Property*

"Read and apply Jill Lublin's strategies in Get Noticed . . . Get Referrals . . . and you are going to get noticed!"

—**Randy Peyser**, author of *The Power of Miracle Thinking*

"Get Noticed . . . Get Referrals *will catapult your career to the next level. Jill shares hundreds of secrets that can help you no matter what your profession.*"

—**Sandra Yancey**, Founder and CEO, eWomenNetwork, Inc.

"Get Noticed . . . Get Referrals *is a clear simple yet powerful guide to all the ways you can get yourself, products, and services right out in front of the publics' eyes.*"

—**David Hancock**, Founder, Morgan James Publishing

get noticed...
get referrals

get noticed...
get referrals

Build Your Client Base And Your Business by Making A Name For Yourself

JILL LUBLIN

with Mark Steisel

New York Chicago San Francisco Lisbon London
Madrid Mexico City Milan New Delhi San Juan
Seoul Singapore Sydney Toronto

1 2 3 4 5 6 7 8 9 0 DOC/DOC 0 9 8

ISBN: 978-0-07-150827-8

MHID: 0-07-150827-9

This publication is designed to provide accurate and authoritative information in regard to the subject matter covered. It is sold with the understanding that the publisher is not engaged in rendering legal, accounting, or other professional service. If legal advice or other expert assistance is required, the services of a competent professional person should be sought.

—*From a Declaration of Principles Jointly Adopted by a Committee of the American Bar Association and a Committee of Publishers and Associations*

McGraw-Hill books are available at special quantity discounts to use as premiums and sales promotions, or for use in corporate training programs. To contact a representative, please visit the Contact Us pages at www.mhprofessional.com.

This book is printed on acid-free paper.

Library of Congress Cataloging-in-Publication Data

Lublin, Jill.
  Get noticed — get referrals : build your client base and your business by making a name for yourself / by Jill Lublin with Mark Steisel.
      p. cm.
  Includes bibliographical references and index.
  ISBN 0-07-150827-9 (alk. paper)
  1. Success in business. 2. Customer relations. 3. Business planning.
  I. Steisel, Mark. II. Title.
  HF5386.L789 2008
  658.8—dc22

                              2008001635

DEDICATION

To God, who makes my life and light possible. May I always spread great messages to make a difference and serve the world. I am continuously grateful for all your blessings.

—Jill Lublin

ACKNOWLEDGMENTS

As THIS BOOK EMPHASIZES, successful endeavors require great teams. For the creation of this book, I had an all-star team, and I'm extremely grateful to each of you for your help!

Thank you for your great support, for selflessly giving me your time, insights, and expertise—you're the best. I greatly appreciate all your hard work, focus, and willingness to share. You are magnificent, I cherish your friendship, and it's always a blessing and a pleasure to work with you.

Thank you to the following friends and colleagues whom we interviewed and whose words have enriched this book. Your knowledge, support, and generosity truly give this book great light:

Kate Adamson
Debbie Allen
Joanne Back
Dick Bruso
Mimi Donaldson
T. Harv Eker
Randy Gilbert
Patti D. Hill
Chet Holmes

Steven Klugman
Mark LeBlanc
Jay Conrad Levinson
Alex Mandosian
Owen Morse
Tommy Newberry
Craig Newmark
David Tyreman
Kym and Sandra Yancey

To Mark Steisel, a collaborator whose excellent work and focus have helped make me who I am today. You're the best!

Thank you to Donya Dickerson, a superb editor and wonderful supporter, and all the wonderful people at McGraw-Hill.

Special kudos to Nancy Ellis, a visionary agent whose commitment has been extraordinary. Nancy saw the possibilities, seized the moment, and made it happen. I appreciate all your support.

I appreciate, love, and acknowledge my parents, Rose Sugerman and Seymour Lublin. Thank you for birthing and loving me into the person I am.

Steve Lillo (www.Planetlink.com)—a playful, fantastic partner—your continuous, unending, unconditional love and support provide a rock-solid foundation for my life.

I also want to acknowledge the varied contributions of many colleagues, mentors, and friends. Thank you one and all:

- Bill and Donna Bauman, founders for the Center for Soulful Living (www.aboutcsl.com). Your wisdom and teaching have greatly influenced my life. Also, Elinor Hall, Kay Whitefeather Robinson, the Bat Clan, and the CSL community. I appreciate and love you all at CSL very much.
- CEO Space (www.CEOSpace.net), the circle of angels, friends, and dream team, particularly, founders Lynn and Berny Dohrmann, two visionaries committed to businesses after hypergrowing.

- Mark LeBlanc (www.SmallBusinessSuccess.com), an expansive mind, unflinching support, and sweetheart who has contributed greatly to my life and success.
- Sincere thanks to Matthew Kent, Rose Singles, Gwenn Stutzman, and other staff, past and present, who have contributed their work, dedication, and passion.
- Jennifer Geronimo, you are a light, and your unwavering support of me over these many years is deeply appreciated. I am grateful for all your commitment and dedication.
- Michelle Rochwarger (www.StrategicResourcesAlliance .com), a dear friend whose profound business advice and friendship means the world.
- Marci Shimoff (www.HappyForNoReason.com), who edited, helped, and loved me in the process. You are a shining star!
- Randy Peyser (www.randypeyser.com), a huge spirit and big heart. I love you!

And finally, thanks to my amazing friends, coaches, and family who bring such support, heart, joy, direction, advice, spirit, and sweetness into my life: T. Harv Eker, Jay Conrad Levinson, Les Hewitt, Natashia Halikowski, Patricia and Vern McDade, John Assaraf, Sue McKinney, Tim Smith, Anne Evanston, Jeanne-Marie Grumet, Michelle Price, Jeff Herzbach, Marie Cooke, Andrea and Reggie Henkart, David and Andrea Lieberstein, Michael Larsen, Elizabeth Pomada, Loral Langemeier, Hollis Polk, Ana Amour, Carol Heller, Jessica Heller Frank, Steve Lublin and family, Jack Lublin, Lynn Fox and family, Sam and Sonya Lillo, Gloria Wilcox, Charles Peri, Jessa Rank, Camille Kurtz, Laurie Moore, Carole Kramer, and all my other angels and guides on this marvelous life journey, both visible and invisible.

CONTENTS

■ ■ ■ ■ ■ ■ ■ ■ ■ ■ ■ ■ ■ ■ ■

get noticed...
get referrals

Introduction

WHEN I LOOK BACK and trace my speaking, writing, and consulting career, I'm fascinated by how it has progressed. If I look at where I started and where I am now, one constant jumps out—how everything I've accomplished has been facilitated by other people.

People have helped me each step of the way. Mr. A introduced me to Ms. B, who recommended me to C Corporation, and it continues to the present day. My career—in fact, my life—has been built through the connections I made and the help of many wonderful people. In the process, I've made many close friends who have enriched every aspect of my life.

Having dear friends in my life has been a true joy because I'm a people person. I love being with and working with other people. I believe that the most important thing in life is to be surrounded by caring people: people whom you love and who love you. To me, nothing is more fulfilling. Working with others makes the day fly by, makes projects more fun, and improves the results. I've been extremely fortunate to have many marvelous people teach me, mentor me, and help me each step of the way.

Now I would like to take the lessons I learned and share them with you.

■ ■ ■ Working with Others

This is my third book. Like both earlier books, *Get Noticed . . . Get Referrals* is about working with others. The process of working with others fascinates, motivates, and energizes me. People's ideas and insights excite me and lift me to higher levels. They send my mind speeding in new directions.

I'm amazed by all the intricacies involved when people work together, the pros and the cons. I've studied them and regularly speak and write about them and have used what I've discovered to build my career. My investigation has taught me what it takes to succeed in business, and promoting oneself tops the list.

The focus of this book is growing your business through self-promotion. Over the years I've found that most people are not good self-promoters. They may have fabulous products or services, but when it comes to selling themselves and their wares, they don't do well. Many are not comfortable, and so they're seldom convincing. Others don't know how to self-promote or are unprepared, and so they get tongue-tied, fearful, and inarticulate. When they finally drum up the courage to speak, they blurt out awkward statements that do more harm than good.

My mission and the purpose of this book are to teach you how to promote yourself, to deliver your message convincingly so that you get noticed and become influential. Your message explains who you are, what you do, and what problems you can solve. Your message and the way you deliver it can be the key to your success.

The information in this book is provided to help you improve your business and your life. Although its main focus is business, I've tried to give you an approach that carries over to all aspects of life.

Whether you are successful usually boils down to whether people trust you to solve their problems. If they are going to pay for your goods or services, they want to know that they can rely on you to deliver the results they need. This book explains how you can build that trust and keep it.

▪ ▪ ▪ This Book

Networking and referral-based business are central themes of this book. They enable people to work successfully with one another and achieve outstanding results. Networking and referrals are natural to most people and are part of their everyday lives. They occur when we recommend a movie, a restaurant, a dentist, or a book.

For most of our lives, all of us have been networking and making and giving referrals. So it's natural for us to extend their use to business because they can make our business lives easier and more efficient, productive, and fun.

A number of exceptional people have contributed stories, insights, and advice to this book. Most of them are colleagues of mine who also happen to be noted experts. All of them have built successful careers via networking and referrals and have studied those subjects in depth. I want to thank them for sharing their knowledge and wisdom so generously.

In this book I am going to teach you the process that has worked for me and many other successful people. I think you will catch on quickly because it's an intuitive, people-oriented, and value-based method that is not just a fad or a quick fix. It's an approach that you can follow throughout your entire career. In addition to helping you improve your business, this process will help you enhance all the other aspects of your life.

Enjoy this book and, more important, use it to produce great happiness and success.

Jill Lublin
September 2007

1

Starting Points

In nature we never see anything isolated, but everything in connection with something else which is before it, beside it, under it and over it.

—Johann Wolfgang von Goethe

This chapter will cover:

- The new environment
- Distinguishing yourself
- Being completely present
- Connecting
- Your outlook
- Having integrity
- Overcoming discomfort

THE BEST WAY TO build or expand your business is to become influential, to convince others that your goods or services can improve their businesses or their lives. To become influential, get noticed. Getting noticed is the most powerful way to drive your business, increase your profitability, and increase your worth.

Getting noticed is a full-time job; it's a continuous process that starts when you slip outside to retrieve the morning paper and doesn't stop until you switch off the lights at night. People watch you from afar; they observe how you act, what you do, how you work, and how well you perform. They listen to what others say about you, and they follow your exploits.

Frequently, people notice you before you spot them or even think of them as potential customers, clients, or referral partners. Everything they see or hear adds to their impression of you and affects the way they judge you. Train yourself to think that you are always being observed because when you drop your guard, even for the briefest moment, that's when they invariably catch you and that will be the impression that sticks—it will preempt all others.

Many people work hard to create a strong first impression and then drop the ball. When they meet others, they always look great and greet them with firm handshakes, dazzling smiles, and mesmerizing opening words, but then they fall flat. Once they think they have them hooked, they relax and don't capitalize on the great impression they have made.

Getting noticed isn't hard, but it usually takes more than one's natural charm. It requires thought, planning, and discipline. You must prepare. It's too important to wing it and not follow through. When you do it right, your life, your business, and your future will improve dramatically. You will perform better and more efficiently, gain confidence, and enjoy greater success.

Before I begin to explain what you should do to get noticed, I want to review some essential points that you must understand. These are the building blocks, the foundation that is necessary for success. Most of these items are value-related, and I believe that is the key to success:

1. The new environment
2. Distinguishing yourself
3. Being completely present
4. Connecting
5. Your outlook
6. Having integrity
7. Overcoming discomfort

■ ■ ■ The New Environment

I'm sure you've noticed how business has changed. We've left the era when companies could sit back, coast on their reputations, and let customers vie to do business with them. Now everything has speeded up and is usually in flux. In business, change is no longer unusual or an isolated event—it's the norm.

To succeed today in business, you can't stand still regardless of how well you are doing. Expect change, continuous change. Expect your markets to be filled with new players and expect more to join every day. Notice how local businesses have gone global and competition has grown fierce. Everyday products are filled with components made all over the globe. Labels, instructions, and manuals are printed in multiple languages. Tactics that served you brilliantly may soon be faded and flat.

With the Internet and instantaneous communications, a new breed of competitors can turn out your core goods and services cheaper, faster, and equally well. As soon as your items hit the street, someone somewhere can duplicate them, beat your price, and deliver his or her version anywhere. To make matters worse, many of them will do *anything* to make a buck.

Along with these changes, marketers have intensified their campaigns. They now hound consumers unrelentingly on every front. Their constant assaults are in full swing 24/7, and that has made consumers wary, even jaded. Since they have heard every pitch and every promise and have been burned, consumers have become deaf to advertisers, hucksters, and promoters and their BS. Buyers today are so guarded and self-protective that getting their attention has become a hurdle that most marketers can't clear.

Cut through the din, the noise, and all that junk mail; adopt new approaches. Stop shouting; someone will always drown you out, plus, you're just adding to the noise. Change your pitch, adjust your tone, alter your voice, rework your message, and design a new plan. Come at them differently with more power, pizzazz, and punch. Work smarter.

Analyze recent changes, examine the competition, and anticipate what the future will bring. Find your special niche, develop solid plans, and work diligently to achieve them. Consistently provide excellence at an accelerated pace. Become customer-oriented. Find shortcuts and get help by building close alliances. Distinguish yourself—*get noticed*.

■ ■ ■ Distinguishing Yourself

Get noticed, but attract the right kind of attention. Forget the myth that "all publicity is good publicity." Think instead of Howard Stern, Paris Hilton, and Britney Spears. Perhaps in the past just being noticed was enough; when people knew your name for any reason, you had arrived. Today, however, brand consciousness and instantaneous communication make building and maintaining strong, positive public opinion a must.

Conversely, bad publicity has become the kiss of death. It's like an oil spill that sludges all in its path. It creates a stain that's hard, if not impossible, to remove. Bad publicity seeps in and tarnishes the name of the polluter; it makes it the object of derision and a bad citizen that everyone wants to go away.

"The best way to get noticed is to always try to help others," Sandra Yancey, founder and CEO of eWomenNetwork, explains. "Reach out and be inquisitive by asking others, 'Who is your ideal client and what is your greatest business challenge today?' People will talk about themselves. When they do, find ways that you can help them. Give them contacts, leads, information, resources, or whatever else they may need."

Adopt a service mentality. If you genuinely try to help others without requesting anything in return, you will distinguish yourself because most people act only when it will benefit them. If you help others, people will appreciate your efforts; they will talk about them and want to help you, and that will make you feel very good.

Build on your uniqueness. "Everything is energy, and the best way to get noticed is to show that your energy is different from everyone else's energy," T. Harv Eker, author of the *New York Times* number one best seller *Secrets of the Millionaire Mind* (HarperCollins,

2005) and president of Peak Potentials Training Inc., stresses. "Find your uniqueness by looking to your strengths, the gifts you have had from the beginning. Find what is normal for you, but not for others."

Lots of people try to come up with hooks that work on a surface level but that don't work well very long. "Be authentic. It must come from deep within you," Eker insists. "If you're authentic, your uniqueness will come through and it will attract the type of people you want to you."

Being Completely Present

Get noticed by being completely present. "Lots of people attend events but are distracted and are not in the present moment," Sandra Yancey finds. "As they talk to you, they scan the room for better opportunities. I call that 'arriving,' not being 'present.'

"When I meet people, it is my responsibility to make the most of it: to be more aware, intentional, cognizant, and present. I must understand that this is a new relationship for me and that I have the choice of acting in ways that take this relationship to the next level."

When you're with others, let them speak. Start by being silent and listening.

Allow them to express themselves fully. Concentrate on what they say, follow their thoughts, and think how you can help them.

Today, people go so fast that they rarely give you their full attention. Distinguish yourself by being completely present, especially in one-to-one situations. When you are completely present, it helps others relax because they know you are listening to them and hearing what they say.

Many people find it hard to communicate. They may not have mastered the social skill of small talk or may freeze when they have to discuss anything of importance. Some are indirect, stutter, sputter, and never get to the point. When they talk about themselves, they talk in circles. They may have great passion, but they can't talk about it or describe it clearly.

Others tend to give far too much information. They may be nervous or not know how to begin. They hem and haw, go into their backgrounds, give rambling preliminaries that go on far too long, or stray far off course.

People also suffer from stage fright. They may to reluctant or afraid to tell you how great they are. If you are successful, you may intimidate them. Many have been taught not to brag, boast, or even talk favorably about themselves.

The key to being completely present is to listen to others without thinking about what you are going to say. When you are completely present, you hear their words and understand their meaning. You are on the same page, hear them out, and don't jump to conclusions. When they have expressed themselves, you can ask intelligent questions and try to get them to give clearer, more informative, or more precise answers.

Being completely present takes practice; it's a process that requires you to do the following:

- Abandon your agenda
- Focus on listening
- Let others speak
- Concentrate on what they are saying
- Interrupt only when you don't understand or to indicate your excitement
- Flow with the conversation
- Be 100 percent there

Connecting

Connecting is the art of building relationships that last. It's the forming of bonds with people that can grow into deeper, closer, more meaningful relationships.

Making close connections is essential because people prefer to work and interact with those with whom they feel connected. They have common interests, feelings, values, and beliefs. They trust those people and want to help them. Instead of concentrating on closing one-time sales, work to build close long-term connections that will endure.

Be honest and build trust. Exaggerating and falsifying may help produce quick sales, but over time that will do you in. Overstating and failing to deliver as promised kill relationships because customers want what they were promised. Few will continue to conduct business with those who have not kept their word. Not delivering precisely as promised is the best way to ruin your reputation and brand.

To create solid connections, follow these suggestions:

- *Perfect your art.* Deliver top quality. Do what you do excellently, as well as it can be done. "There is no substitute for quality," T. Harv Eker states. "If the quality you provide is outstanding, you don't have to do lots of networking. People will network for you. They will tell others about you and recommend you. People love to refer others to those who provide the top quality." It makes them look good.
- *Stick to the facts.* It's easy to exaggerate and promise more than you can deliver, but it doesn't pay. Be honest. Connect with potential customers by telling them the results your goods and services have achieved. Better yet, document the results, put on demonstrations, and show them proof. Provide them with endorsements from satisfied customers; take them to sites where your goods or services are in operation with other customers. Then explain to your prospects exactly how you can help them.
- *Don't promise too much,* especially if you may not be able deliver. Be completely honest. It's better to lose a sale and stay on good terms with the prospect than to land the sale and alienate the customer. If your honesty costs you a deal, think of it this way: The customer may remember your truthfulness and call on you again. However, if you overinflate or fail to deliver, your future with that prospect

will be doomed, over, kaput. Plus, aggrieved customers tend to tell their friends about their dissatisfaction, especially when they feel they were deceived intentionally.

- *When you're looking for business, offer your goods or services at an attractive price.* Be fair and don't gouge; build trust. Give potential customers a price incentive for giving you their business. When you have performed well for them, you can use them as a showcase to sell to future customers. You also will have forged connections with satisfied customers who will give you repeat business and recommend you to others.

Obtaining repeat business is highly cost-effective. It runs about 80 percent less than the expense of attracting new clients. Dick Bruso, the founder of Heard Above the Noise (www.heardabove .com), points out that working through referrals gives you more time. Most businesspeople spend an average of 25 to 30 percent of their time trying to reach those they need to conduct their business. In contrast, a person who works by referrals spends only about 5 percent of his or her time getting to those he or she wants to meet.

Ask satisfied customers to give you endorsements or letters of commendation. Have them write on their letterheads how excellently you performed. Post the commendations on your Web site, hang copies in your office, and keep them in a scrapbook you can show potential customers. Insert them in your brochures and sales materials.

■ ■ ■ Your Outlook

Remember back in school how different personalities emerged and distinguished themselves. Every school had characters such as the nerd, the rocker, the jock, the babe, and the brain. Yet the one we tend to remember most fondly is the clown.

We all noticed the clown because he (sometimes, she) made us laugh. He connected with everyone through his humor; he made everything funny. The clown could make the most ordinary situation, the gravest circumstance, and the blandest personality absolutely hysterical. During the darkest moments, his quips broke the tension and lightened the mood. Humor was his focus, his outlook, his forte. His wit was what distinguished him and the way he connected.

Great networkers also have a special outlook. Like the clown who instinctively looks for humor, networkers are programmed to connect with people. Great networkers constantly try to meet new people, learn all about them, and link them so that they can build close, mutually beneficial relationships.

Distinguish yourself and boost your business by developing a connecting attitude. Be pleasant, friendly, and fun. People want to be with and do business with those they like, not with grouches.

"If you walk around like you have been weaned on a pickle, no one will want to do business with you," observes Mark LeBlanc, president of Small Business Success and author of *Growing Your Business!* (Beaver's Pond Press, 1999). "Accept some of your shortcomings or failings in the early stages and practice strengthening what I call 'the next muscle in your brain.' When someone isn't interested in what you have or do, go on to the next one," LeBlanc suggests.

Train yourself to be a connector; develop a connecting frame of mind by constantly thinking in terms of those with whom you can connect. Here's how to proceed.

Make two lists:

1. List people you would like to meet.
   a. Create a plan to meet your targets.
   b. Identify those who could introduce you to your targets or people who could connect you to them.
   c. List what you have in common with your targets, such as common:
      i. Friends
      ii. Businesses
      iii. Backgrounds
      iv. Interests
      v. Values and beliefs

2. List people whom you could connect with one another. List what they have in common:
   a. Friends
   b. Businesses
   c. Backgrounds
   d. Interests
   e. Values and beliefs
3. Create a plan to connect those individuals.

> Connecting is addictive. When you make a strong connection it's so satisfying that you can't wait to do it again. It's also rewarding because people are grateful for your efforts on their behalf. Successful connections motivate; they make you focus more on connecting and bringing more people together.

Since connectors are always trying to make matches, they become possibility people. Possibility people explore, try, and make things happen. They push the limits and don't immediately accept no for an answer.

Possibility people stand out because they're optimistic and more likely to achieve. They also tend to be creative, resourceful, and inspirational. If you want to increase your business referrals, develop a connecting outlook.

▪ ▪ ▪ Having Integrity

People have become much more environmentally concerned. It's as if they suddenly agreed that we have to work together to save our planet. This new thinking is being impressed on school kids, and so tomorrow it will be the order of the day. Simultaneously, it is being featured prominently in the media and on the Internet and adopted by the corporate world. Businesses that traditionally resisted it are going green. People everywhere seem to have joined in a crusade to work together and save our world.

This greater environmental consciousness is integrity-based. It centers on being responsible, doing what is right and necessary for humanity, not just for oneself. After years of abuses, Enron, government scandals, and shameless profiteers have triggered a new ethic of service and working toward the greater good. The public has become more idealistic, more focused on values, not just the bottom line. Its values have changed.

The green movement and the spirit fueling it have trickled into business. Companies now see that they can profit by cleaning up their operations and producing environmentally friendly products. They are announcing it in their advertising, public relations, products, corporate sponsorships, and charitable endeavors. And the movement is only going to grow, so get on the bandwagon and align yourself with these increasingly admired values.

"If you have integrity, you will get noticed," T. Harv Eker believes. "So few people have integrity that if you have it, you will stand out. Keep your word, be reliable, do what you said you would, overdeliver."

Businesses that last are based on integrity. They always do a great job, strike fair deals, and treat people well. They exist to serve their customers, not just their shareholders. Reliability and value are the foundation, the base, from which businesses must build because their customers want to deal with people on whom they can depend. They don't want to give their money to companies they don't respect.

Treat your clients and customers well and always do what is right for them. Remember, there is no right way to do the wrong thing.

Set a high standard of professionalism. Distinguish yourself by consistently performing excellently, without delays, excuses, or broken promises. Build a reputation for excellence.

"There is no substitute for quality," T. Harv Eker believes. "Massive quality is so rare, that if you provide it, people will talk about you. You must have a product or service that is a 12 out of 10; you must be a 12 out of 10. People will talk about and recommend you because they love to tell others about something good. There is no substitute for the quality of what you do and how you do it. If you have a great item but don't market it well, they will also talk about that. If you have a great package but what it contains is garbage, people will notice and talk about it."

When you have built a track record for being honest and dependable and providing great quality and value, announce it to the world. When you do, you will be reciting facts, not selling. Your history of integrity and top performance will make people take notice, listen, and want to conduct business with you.

"Your job is to make yourself so good at whatever you say, do, or offer that people will seek you out," Jay Conrad Levinson, the father of Guerrilla Marketing, stresses. "The key is not trying to find people who you want to work with, it's making yourself so attractive that they will want to work with you. Make people seek you out."

According to Levinson, "When most people network, they talk about themselves and hand out business cards. However, they should be asking questions, finding out about people, and collecting their business cards. Everyone who networks wants to find people to work with, so they will pick those who stand out. Make yourself so fascinating, so compelling, that people seek you out."

Examine your position in your community. Don't be out only for yourself. See how you can be a part of something larger and greater. When you do, it can take you in exciting new directions that may have great and lucrative possibilities for your growth. You can attract new and powerful people, people with ideas and vision who will want to associate, trailblaze, and do business with you.

Craigslist is admired for its integrity. "We are all very committed and we follow through, but I don't feel that we are noble," Craigslist founder Craig Newmark revealed. "Following through and commitment is a big deal. Many companies talk about their high standards, but they don't mean it. Distinguish yourself by listening and following through."

■ ■ ■ Overcoming Discomfort

Most people are uncomfortable promoting themselves. Debbie Allen, the author of *Confessions of Shameless Self Promoters* (McGraw-

Hill, 2006) and a professional business speaker, polled thousands of members of her audiences. She found that 85 percent were uncomfortable with the idea of promoting themselves. Their feelings stemmed from their being taught that modesty is a virtue, and they never boast or brag.

The noted speaker Mimi Donaldson (www.mimidonaldson.com), the author of *Bless Your Stress: It Means You're Still Alive!* (Yes! Press, 2001), adds, "When Mother said, 'Don't toot your own horn,' Mother was wrong. We were taught that the key was to work hard—if you worked hard, you would be noticed. However, when you work hard, what you get is more work. So, to prevent yourself from being completely swamped and to do what you want, you have to toot your own horn."

"Women have it a little harder because they were raised with the admonition that it is not ladylike to toot your own horn," Donaldson notes. "So women need a little extra push. Fortunately, over the past twenty years, we've done a much better job. I've watched women grow, and one of the main barometers is how good they are becoming at self-promotion."

To overcome their reluctance to self-promote, Debbie Allen teaches people to promote themselves in the service of others. "If they believe that they are helping others, it eases their guilt about promoting themselves and they can self-promote," she says.

■ ■ ■ CONNECTING LINK ■ ■ ■

If self-promotion makes you uncomfortable, state the facts without embellishment or exaggeration. Distinguish yourself from marketers who get so caught up in the heat of a potential sale that they cross the line between the truth and wishful thinking. In their zeal to make a sale, they say whatever they feel is necessary to close the deal, even if it may not be completely true. They may inflate their experience, past results, and capabilities.

Distinguish yourself by always telling the truth.

"Provided they are unselfish and come from the heart. When they come from the heart, what they say will be authentic and will not seem pushy or like a sales pitch."

Nervousness also plagues people. "I'm nervous before every show," Owen Morse of the comedy juggling team The Passing Zone reveals. "If you're not afraid to get up in front of people and do your thing, you've gotten yourself in too much of a comfort zone. You're not trying something new, and you may be riding that line of phoning it in. If you're not nervous or concerned about how it will play, you're not going to challenge yourself or to look for opportunities to connect with people and grow."

Action Plan

1. Decrease the discomfort of praising yourself by creating a statement of self-praise.

   _____

   _____

   _____

2. List how you can be more completely present.

   _____

   _____

   _____

   _____

   _____

3. List the names of people you would like to meet.

   _____

   _____

   _____

   _____

4. List the names of individuals who could connect you with the people you want to meet.

   _____

   _____

   _____

   _____

   _____

2

Getting It Straight

This chapter will cover:

- Interview checklist
- Informing clients and customers
- Putting it in writing
- Confirming agreements
- Terms

GET NOTICED BY BEING professional. Please your clients and customers by learning what they want and always delivering it. People have many choices and can give their business to many companies. Consistently provide what they want or they won't continue to do business with you, and they definitely won't recommend you to others.

When sellers court customers, they make many promises. Words are bandied about; expectations are formed, as are misconceptions. Misunderstandings can undermine relationships, so avoid them by identifying everyone's expectations as soon as possible. On every project, find out what each of you expects to receive and agrees to give.

Learn what each customer wants. You can't meet customers' expectations if you don't know what they want. When I work with a client, my first question is, "What do you want and what are your objectives?" When I get the answer, I know exactly what I must do and where I must focus. I make a list of everything my client wants and read it to him or her. We clarify anything that isn't clear and make changes and additions. Then I create a plan that details how I will work with my client to accomplish all of his or her goals.

Treat your clients and customers as you would like to be treated. When problems arise, as they will, immediately inform the customer and clearly explain what will be involved in resolving the situation. Admit your mistakes and don't try to cover them up. Then do your best to fix them.

When you're in the business of serving or supplying others, your primary job is to deliver what they want. However, parties frequently don't agree on what each of them is supposed to give and receive. Or, as projects progress, the parties may lose sight of precisely what was agreed to.

Before you begin working on a project, know what's involved. Clarify everyone's duties, responsibilities, and expectations. If you're not sure, ask questions until it's clear. Set schedules with precise deadlines, specify payment times and amounts, and know exactly what you're supposed to give and what you are to receive. This knowledge will create the foundation on which to build a solid working relationship.

Before I agree to work with clients, I conduct interviews with them. At the interviews, we speak at length to clarify exactly what they want and precisely what they expect. Our conversations are full and open and set the tone for the work we will be doing together. They help us learn how to communicate clearly with each other, and that helps greatly as projects proceed.

In our conversations, we specifically agree on what each expects to get and receive. We identify the outcome that will be provided, set target dates for all the important steps, and define the standards that must be met. Then we work together to create a viable plan to achieve them.

Owen Morse and Jon Wee are partners in the comedy juggling team The Passing Zone. To make their performances sparkle, they make sure that they understand who their clients are and what they need. A month before each performance, they conduct a conference call with the client and ascertain who it is, what it needs, who the audience is, what issues and problems the audience may be facing, and what of significance has happened with or to them recently. Then Morse and Wee use that information to customize their performance for that audience.

■ ■ ■ Interview Checklist

When I interview potential clients, I try to leave nothing to chance. I focus on gathering enough information to give me a clear understanding of what they want and expect.

To make sure nothing falls through the cracks, I follow a checklist that I've developed over the years. That checklist helps me learn about potential clients and their needs. As I run down the items on the list, I get an idea of what each project entails, what I will have to do, and what the prospect needs and expects.

These interviews set the tone for my relationships with my clients. They teach me how they communicate, negotiate, and respond. By the end of an interview, I usually can tell how well we can communicate, whether the person and his or her expectations are reasonable, and if I want to work with him or her.

My interviews and the effort I make show my clients that I'm professional, demonstrating to them how focused I am on discovering what they want and delivering it to them. The process helps enlist their complete cooperation and ensures the project's success.

If I don't feel good about a potential client or project, I will not accept the work. I trust my instincts and carefully follow them. If I have strong feelings, I know that somewhere down the line they will prove to be correct.

My client interview checklist for my public relations business is reprinted below. Note that it was created for my public relations and counseling business. When you write a client interview checklist, adapt it so that it will disclose specific information you need for your business.

Client Interview Checklist

☐ What problem does the client address?

_____

_____

_____

_____

☐ What solutions does the client offer?

_____

_____

_____

_____

☐ What secondary problems does the client address?

_____

_____

_____

_____

☐ What secondary solutions does the client offer?

_____

_____

_____

_____

_____

☐ Which of my techniques might help the client?

_____

_____

_____

_____

☐ What are the three primary objectives he or she would like to accomplish?

_____

_____

_____

☐ How strong is the client's
- Message?
  - What does it need?

    _____

    _____

    _____

- Presentation?
  - What does it need?

    _____

    _____

    _____

☐ Review the client's program and find what dollars are being thrown away.

_____

_____

_____

☐ Define the best audiences and niches.

_____

_____

_____

_____

☐ Expand and develop unique, creative ways to reach new audiences.

_____

_____

_____

_____

_____

☐ Create a bio that positions the client as an expert. Include:

_____

_____

_____

_____

_____

☐ Create an announcement. Include:

_____

_____

_____

_____

_____

☐ Write a powerful press release. Include:

_____

_____

_____

_____

_____

☐ Identify the target media.

_____

_____

_____

_____

_____

☐ Write a media script. Include:

_____

_____

_____

_____

_____

☐ Write media follow-ups. Include:

_____

_____

_____

_____

_____

☐ Write follow-ups for the client's support team. Include:

_____

_____

_____

_____

_____

☐ Media training

☐ Fee arrangement:

_____

_____

_____

_____

☐ Special items:

_____

_____

_____

_____

_____

■ ■ ■ Informing Clients and Customers

Be clear about what you will provide so that clients do not make assumptions or have expectations that you can't satisfy. Try to clarify precisely the services you will provide.

To explain your services, give prospective clients a descriptive sheet that describes your programs and what you provide. Instead of relying on verbal statements to detail your services, give prospective clients written documents that they can read, consider, and use as a guide to question you. When prospective clients read your descriptive sheets, you will be able to have more focused and productive meetings. You also will have fewer misunderstandings.

I also send my explanation sheets to my network and referral partners and ask them for materials describing their goods or services. We also discuss how each of us prefers to operate. That way, I am able to make the best matches and not refer people to contacts who are not suited to handle their projects.

An explanation sheet shows that you are professional. Add blurbs: quotes from satisfied clients stating how helpful you were to them. "Working with Jane was like working with a top New York agency. . . ." Include testimonials. Make clarifying explanations the start of your relationship with clients. It's vital in building close working relationships.

Write an explanation of your services to give to your clients. Fully list what you plan to provide. Explanations will help you avoid subsequent misunderstandings and unwarranted expectations.

■ ■ ■ Putting It in Writing

The best way to clarify your arrangements with clients is to put them in writing. Written agreements also keep most clients' expectations in check and provide a professional basis for the relationship.

> ■ ■ ■ **CONNECTING LINK** ■ ■ ■
>
> I always try to have written agreements with my clients. The biggest problems I've encountered in business occurred when I worked without written agreements and did not carefully read those which someone rushed me into. Even when agreements exist, they are always subject to interpretation, as is virtually everything in life. But reducing the basic items of agreement to writing can eliminate many problems later on.

In agreements, define anything that isn't clear. After I speak with a potential client, I send a quick e-mail that outlines our agreement. I act promptly, when our understanding is still fresh in our minds. If I remember anything incorrectly or miss important points, the client will have the opportunity to tell or correct me.

I prefer to send e-mail because it's easy for people to respond to. Also, it's informal. Other people favor letters of agreement or formal written contracts. The method is secondary; the primary objective should be to provide clarity and define the parameters of the relationship.

Since I prefer e-mail, my agreements tend to turn into a series of e-mails stating what each of us will give and receive. I print each e-mail and place it in a file that I can access quickly when questions arise.

Many people hate contracts. Frequently, they are so excited about the project that they dive right into it without discussing everyone's expectations and clearly defining them. These people may fear that if they start hammering out all the details, the deal will go down the drain. Don't fall into that trap. Clarify your agreements in writing.

Reducing your agreements to writing makes good business sense:

- It minimizes misunderstandings.
- It provides a sign that you are professional. It sends the message that you know what you are doing and understand all the elements that will be involved.
- It helps you refine and clarify your understanding.
- It helps you think the project through, identify your needs, and list the steps you will have to take.
- It gives the other person the chance to express any differences of opinion that might exist.

Be clear on what you're going to give and receive and be sure that all major items have been included. When you discuss the items of agreement, it gives you a subtle way to blow your own horn and get noticed. It allows you to state what you can deliver, including items that your client didn't expect or even think about. Besides showing your professionalism, you can demonstrate that you provide excellent value.

■ ■ ■ Confirming Agreements

As soon as possible, confirm all verbal agreements. Take the initiative and contact the other party while the terms are still fresh in your minds. Confirm the agreement even if you plan to execute a formal contract so that there are no questions about the basic deal.

In early June, Stan, a motion picture producer, called me. He said that he was interested in working with me on a project that would not start until the fall. However, he called me then to make contact, introduce himself, and ask a few preliminary questions. He then inquired about my experience promoting films and working with film publicists. He seemed pleased with my answers and concluded by saying that he would get back in touch with me by August 1.

I answered Stan's questions, and we had a pleasant, productive conversation. After he hung up, I sent him the following e-mail along with my explanation sheet:

Dear Stan,

Thank you for your telephone call. I enjoyed speaking with you and hope that we get the opportunity to work together. I look forward to hearing from you after August 1.

Your film project sounds fascinating, and I would enjoy exploring ways in which I could consult on the planning and running of your publicity campaign. Attached is my Explanation Sheet that describes my services. Please feel free to contact me if you have any questions.

Thanks again.

Jill

I then placed an entry on my calendar for August 1 to remind me to contact Stan if I had not heard from him by then. When he did not call, I called him, and he was grateful. He referred to my e-mail and raised a few questions, which we discussed, and we agreed to work together. We concluded our agreement in no time flat and began an enjoyable, productive relationship.

I believe in sending short, direct e-mails. Most people skim e-mails and don't read them closely, so I make sure that mine are brief and to the point, usually no more than two or three sentences.

Of course, you may work differently, and you should make it clear to your clients how you prefer to work. People must know what they can expect when they work with you. If they are shelling out money, they have that right. Many people concentrate so much on selling themselves and telling prospects about themselves that they don't clarify what the prospect needs and explain what he or she will get. They should state, "Here are the terms, and here is what you will receive."

If you provide intangibles, tell the prospect exactly what they are. For example, I help clients overcome their anxiety about introducing themselves and making a powerful first impression. I don't usually specify that or other intangibles that I will provide in written agreements unless they are the main focus of the project. However, during our conversations, I tell my clients, "I will help you overcome your fears so that you can deliver your message more effectively."

When you describe the intangible items you will provide, they will become more concrete objectives. When your clients understand what you will be trying to achieve, they will work harder to accomplish them. For many clients, they will become targets, tangible goals that they will work to attain. Providing this important information will help you and your clients communicate better and create strong, productive working relationships.

When I speak with prospects by phone, I work from my description sheet, which I use as a checklist. Then, when I send prospects a copy of my description sheet, I again clarify precisely what they can expect to receive from me. During phone conversations, I don't recite directly from the description sheet because I won't want to sound canned or stale. I use the sheet as a checklist to make sure I cover all the important points.

Being professional helps raise you above the crowd. It distinguishes you and gets you noticed in a highly favorable way. It boosts your brand, helping you make connections, build relationships, and get more referrals.

■ ■ ■ Terms

Language can be unclear, so define all key terms to make sure that everyone is speaking the same language. For example, I tell people that I am going to help them create a message that the media will say yes to. Many people may not understand what I mean by the word *message*, so I define it for them. Their message is a one- or two-sentence introduction that explains the benefits they will provide.

On a basic, core level, you must have a rapport with those with whom you work. That means hearing them; understanding their language, styles, and values; and realizing who they are. Get context and work on levels that they will understand and accept.

If you're representing a chic, elegant woman, it's essential to understand what will satisfy her and what she won't like. From her demeanor and appearance you can infer that she expects precision, formality, and grace. Although informal, relaxed, or funky presentations may be fine with other clients, they probably will be inappropriate for a client with her refined, sophisticated taste.

Jeannie, a technical writer, specializes in simplifying highly complex information. She can make the most difficult, dense, and confusing material easily understandable. Jeannie was hired by Jackson, who was fascinated by nuance, subtlety, and hidden meanings. Jackson always found everything to have a deeper, more complex, or ambiguous meaning. When Jeannie and Jackson worked together, it was a disaster. They engaged in a mental tug-of-war with each of them pulling in the opposite direction. Although they liked each other and compromised to accommodate each other, they never were able to reach a happy medium and could not work together successfully.

Frequently, we turn to people who are our opposites to see the other side, to take us places we could never reach by ourselves. Although it's often beneficial to get their insights, many people simply can't hear other approaches or truly don't want to go that way.

Every industry, every profession, and many businesses have their own language. They use shorthand, abbreviations, and terms of art. As a result, they often speak in code. Since everyone in their group understands them, they assume that everyone else does too.

I worked on a project with a large shipping company, and when I met with their personnel, I couldn't understand what they were saying. I continually asked them for clarification, but they were so focused on technical information, they never realized that they were not being clear. They were at work, and everyone at work spoke and understood their jargon. The fact that I was an outsider never dawned on them. The consulting work I performed helped them create sound bites that everyone could understand.

Be cautious. Don't talk in code and be sure that the other person understands you. Examine your words; make sure they are clear. I go back to the "five-year-old" rule and ask whether I can be understood by a kindergartener.

In communicating, the most important objective is to make yourself understood. Smart and accomplished individuals are especially prone to using jargon and big, uncommon words. They know what they're talking about and assume that others also do. However, jargon confuses most people and turns them off. Unfortunately, some people use such lingo to impress, but it usually has the opposite effect because it bores or confuses their listeners.

Break your use of code by speaking with people outside your field, people who will tell you the truth. Ask them directly if they understood you, if you were completely clear, and how you could have said it better. Identify your mistakes and don't repeat them. Getting external feedback forces you to engage with people outside your field and see if you can get your message across clearly and convincingly.

When both you and your clients or customers clearly understand the terms of your arrangements, your projects will run more smoothly and you will have fewer misunderstandings. When your clients and customers get what they expected, they will be satisfied and more likely to recommend you to others.

Action Plan

1. Adapt my client interview checklist for your business. List the questions you would ask.

   _____

   _____

   _____

   _____

   _____

   _____

2. Why it is important to state the terms of an agreement in writing?

   _____

   _____

   _____

   _____

3. Compose an e-mail that confirms what you just agreed to during a meeting.

   _____

   _____

   _____

   _____

4. In what areas could you increase your professionalism when you perform?

   _____

   _____

   _____

   _____

3

You Can't Do It Alone

This chapter will cover:

- Teamwork
- Forming networks
- Remaining fresh
- Attitude
- The Power Referral Program
- Referral arrangements
- Premarketing

WHEN I FIRST STARTED my business, I felt that I should be able to run every aspect of it myself. After all, I reasoned, it was my business and I should handle whatever was involved. Soon, I found that although I had skills, I also had big, gaping holes, areas where I was deficient. I knew publicity and I had a talent for connecting people, but I didn't understand what a P&L (profit and loss statement) was and why I needed one.

I had to get training to learn the language; find out what was involved, what I could deduct, and what was taxable; and everything I was required to do. Then I had to learn how to keep records, fill out forms, and make timely payments.

Much of what I had to learn didn't come easy. I didn't like it, and it took valuable time away from the productive, enjoyable activities that were building my business. The first chance I got, I hired a bookkeeper and then a CPA.

I learned a big lesson that has carried over to other aspects of my business. That experience taught me to look for and identify areas where I need help. As a result, I now hire assistants, writers, editors, graphic designers, people to help me with my speaking career, and people to help me sell my speaking career. Since I travel a lot, I work with an agency that handles whatever I need.

I appreciate experts and their wealth of knowledge. They have helped me over hurdles and taught me a great deal. They've also saved me loads of time. Look for the best people in your areas of need; besides getting expert help, you can learn a great deal from them, and they can be a superb source of referrals.

▪ ▪ ▪ Teamwork

To succeed in business, it takes teamwork; you can't make it without help. The day of the Lone Ranger is long gone, and even he had a trusty sidekick. Business is now a team sport.

Think how many credits run at the end of a motion picture; they can scroll for dozens of screens. The people in pit crews at NASCAR races and those who back up the star attractions at live performances are only the ones you see; many more work behind the scenes.

Recently, I attended *The Late Show with David Letterman*, which was a hoot. Throughout the show, Letterman occupied center stage while an extensive team, which viewers generally don't see, constantly buzzed around him. In addition to the band and his cast of on-camera players, Letterman has dozens of writers and production and technical people whom the audience never sees.

Networks are teams: groups of people who help one another achieve their objectives. Each network member has his or her own networks. So thus, when your network gets a new member, it also receives that member's network and everyone who belongs to it. Every member of your network and your members' networks is a potential source of referrals, as is each person to whom he or she refers you. When more people are involved, the number of referrals and the new business you receive can soar. Here are some of the benefits of networks:

- Working with others can make your tasks easier, more pleasant, and more enjoyable.
- Networks give you access to people with whom you can confer and strategize.
- Network members become your friends; they can introduce you to new people, developments, and interests that can extend your reach.

Business is complex. It has numerous facets, many of which you may not know that well. You may be a great administrator, a financial genius, or a manufacturing whiz but know little or nothing about sales, personnel, or product development. Fortunately, experts are available in each of your weak areas and can be added to your team.

"Now women are getting into working more in teams," Mimi Donaldson declares. "Finally, women are getting smart about it and are associating with highly competent women who make as much money as they do. And it's paying off."

A little help can go a long way. Shoshana Bennett, the author of *Postpartum Depression for Dummies* (Wiley, 2006), was struggling to do everything herself, but she never had enough time. I persuaded her to get a virtual assistant to help her answer correspondence, make calls, send invoices, set appointments, and maintain her calendar. Within days, the difference was apparent. By delegating less important tasks to her assistant, Shoshana was able to concentrate on more important activities and accomplish two to three times more.

Forming Networks

We all have networks. They consist of everyone we know: our friends, family, and business associates. Our doctors, dentists, dry cleaners, mechanics, and CPAs are also members of our networks.

Networks are an invaluable source of referrals. Referral expert Joanne Black, the author of *No More Cold Calling* (Warner Business Books, 2006), notes that when you get clients or customers through referrals, the following things happen:

1. You are presold. They have heard about and want to work with you.
2. You have credibility.
3. You have trust.
4. A definite need for your goods or services exists, and the contact wants to meet with you.
5. The sales cycle is shortened dramatically.
6. You can ace out the competition.
7. You get more business. Most of the time, you land more than 50 percent of the contacts you meet, and the number frequently exceeds 70 percent.

Identify Your Existing Network
- List everyone you know who could help you.
- Next to each name write:
  - What he or she does
  - How he or she could help you
- Underline the names of those who you think could be the most helpful in expanding your horizons. Make them your A Group: the people who could help you the most and with whom you want to solidify your relationship.

Networks are reciprocal arrangements. Build networks with partners who will refer business to you and will always do an excellent job for those you recommend. Align yourself with people who have the following characteristics:

1. *Are like you and have similar values and goals.* Having similar values is essential because it gives you a better chance of being on the same page, speaking the same language, and working well together. When you have the same values, it helps build trust. If your values differ, conflicts inevitably will arise. People who understand my values know what is important to me. The more I insist on working with people who share my values, the easier, more successful, and more enjoyable my life becomes. Identify your values so that you can find them in others.

2. *Can fill in your gaps.* We all have shortcomings: areas in which we are not accomplished. We also can't do everything, although we often try. Compensate for your weaknesses by aligning yourself with people who excel in areas in which you fall short. For example, I am a strong promoter; that's my personality. I need to work with analysts who keep me focused on business and the bottom line. However, I also want those people to share my values and understand what's important to me.

3. *Are on a higher level.* Notch it up; work with people who are smarter, more experienced, more accomplished, and better connected than you—people from whom you can learn. "You become who you associate with the most," Debbie Allen counsels. "So if you want to get to a higher level, be with people who are on a higher level. Most people don't. They stay at the same level and never move past their old friends and associates."

"Connecting with people who have more influence and success raises your skill level and creates new opportunities for you," Sandra Yancey, founder and president of eWomenNetwork, discloses. "You can only raise your game if you play with superior players. You need to place that stress on yourself to get better. It's critical for people to search for ways to build relationships and associate with those who have more, who do more, and have accomplished more."

Find the best coaches, teachers, instructors, and mentors. At first, working with experts may be awkward; you may feel that you are in over your head. Usually, that's just growing pains. Before long you will get up to speed. As you work with more talented individuals, educate yourself by listening, reading, and taking courses so that you can absorb what they give you. Be patient and willing to work your way up step by step; understand that you are involved in a process. Don't try to jump from the bottom straight to the top because you could have a long, hard fall.

"Stay away from 'dream-stealers,'" Debbie Allen urges. "They are people who are negative and will hold you back. If you do something that makes them feel uncomfortable, something that they wouldn't do, they will discourage and try to stop you."

"Take inventory of the people you hang around with," Sandra Yancey suggests. "Unless you look, you can't imagine how much time you may be giving to people who are not serving you well. They are not supporting your efforts, and they are draining you of your dreams. Quietly fire those dream drainers because you only have so much time. Don't let those who are stuck in misery lure you onto their team."

Concentrate on working with referral partners who consistently can send you quality business. Make sure you love what you do and spend your time with the best people in your field.

When you start building networks, start close to home; build a strong home base. Review your business records and identify those with whom you could form strategic alliances. Ask your clients, customers, vendors, and service providers for referrals. They know how well you perform.

▪ ▪ ▪ Remaining Fresh

Networks are constantly in flux: People come, go, and move in different directions. They get tired, bored, burned out. Changes in their lives may prevent them from helping you. Your relationship with them may be wonderful for a while and then become less productive or peter out. Circumstances change; solutions that always used to hit the mark may no longer work.

At times, you have to make changes; some of your network partners may not be performing well or may be holding you back. The referrals they make may not be helping your career. If they no longer provide quality leads and referrals, you may have to shift them to your friends list from your business associates list.

To operate most efficiently, networks continually need new blood. New members introduce new outlooks, contacts, and approaches that can prevent groups from becoming stale. Continually monitor and check whether each of your relationships is producing what you want. Ask, "Is this person still serving the cause? Should I move him or her to another area or lessen my reliance on him or her?

Frequently, an internal alarm sounds to tell you that you have outgrown someone or something and that changes are needed. Unfortunately, most people let problems go on too long before addressing them, and suddenly they wake up and find that they're

■ ■ ■ **CONNECTING LINK** ■ ■ ■

Your networks must center on you; they must serve your needs. Don't approach networks as if they were civic, community, religious, or social organizations that are dedicated to accomplishing a common goal. Such organizations succeed because their members give of themselves for the greater good.

Your networks must serve you. Build a team filled with individuals who have the types of talents, expertise, and contacts that will help you. Then support them, give generously to them, and send them referrals to forge strong bonds. Reciprocity and mutual giving are the backbone of strong, successful networks.

stuck in the middle of a real mess. As a result, they are caught by surprise and don't have as much time to respond to and deal with it.

Review your list:

- Determine which network members are strong and which could be improved.
- Examine how you can strengthen your circle and make it wider, broader, and more productive. Identify areas in which you could use help.
- Find potential cross-promotional possibilities. For example, if you are a CPA, network with tax attorneys. If you are an accident attorney or own a body shop, work with insurance brokers.
- Then start identifying individuals who could be stronger partners.

When you recruit new network partners, be sure that they agree with your values. This will make the relationship more enjoyable and successful, and in addition, you will be judged by those with whom you associate. If one of your associates behaves questionably, his or her actions could reflect on you; they could influence others negatively, tarnish your reputation, and hold you back.

▧ ▧ ▧ Attitude

Ask yourself if you need to adjust your attitude. If you do, assume the role of the person you want to be, a person who already has achieved success.

"Always self-promote 24/7 and be very intentional," Tommy Newberry, the author of *The 4:8 Principle* (Tyndale House Publishers, 2007), states. "First, know what your end game is, where you want to be, how you want to be perceived, at least ten years down the road if not twenty or thirty. The clearer you know at the outset what you want your life and career to be, the easier it will be figure out how you should promote yourself."

According to Newberry, "Aligning your habits with the person you want to be is the first step in making yourself attractive to others." Exude confidence and competence, not doubt. "Don't use wishy-washy words like 'hope to' and 'if all works out well,'" Newberry warns. "Claim the future as a certainty. Act now with the confidence that you would have if you already accomplished you biggest goals."

"Don't say, 'I want to be a software entrepreneur,'" Newberry advises. "Declare, 'I'm the CEO of ABC Software Company.' Think that way. You don't have to verbalize that attitude to everyone, but walk around and act like it already occurred. If you imagine that it happened and act as if that is your reality, people will pick up on it. However, if you hesitate or show doubt, you will be less attractive to them. Create the right attitude mentally before you create it in reality."

Minimize the risk by being willing to pay the price; work hard to become the person you want to be. "If you know that you are going to back up your words with hard work, it will give you the confidence to act the part," Newberry observes.

■ ■ ■ The Power Referral Program

Branding expert Dick Bruso has developed the Power Referral Program. His system is premised on the belief that people do business with you for four reasons:

- They trust you.
- They like you.
- You are competent in your area of expertise.
- You have integrity.

Here's how Bruso's Power Referral Program works:

1. Create a list of 10 people you love and who love you regardless of whether they are in the business you are trying to reach. Select those who trust you, like you, and

believe that you're competent and have integrity. It's all about mutual respect.

2. Meet with each of them individually.

3. Tell them the types of overall markets you want to penetrate, for example, sole proprietors, small businesses, corporations, partnerships, nonprofit organizations, or educational institutions.

4. Then zero in more closely. Identify the specialty area you want to reach, such as financial services, health care, human resources, or computer technology. If you are in the financial services industry, state that you want referrals in banking, investing, financial planning, insurance, real estate, and so on.

5. Know the positions of the people you want to meet and ask your contacts if they know people in those positions who could help your business move forward. For example, tell them that you would like to meet decision makers such as CEOs, CFOs, purchasing agents, and human resource supervisors. When in doubt, go to the top person. The more specific you are about your targets, the better off you will be. For example, explain that you want to reach small businesses, single proprietors, corporations, governments, nonprofits, or educational institutions.

Bruso stresses that it's essential to identify clearly the people you wish to meet, because your contact may know someone who fits the bill. Unfortunately, most people are not specific enough. They also make the mistake of assuming that if someone is in a particular field or category, that's all that person is. However, people are multifaceted and have many contacts, Bruso points out. Your auto mechanic may service a top estate attorney's car. "People have multiple spheres of interest," Bruso explains. "The more you talk, the more common areas you will find which you may have never even thought about."

6. State the personal aspects you would like. For example, does the person have integrity? Is he or she dependable, inventive, kind, and fun to work with?

According to Bruso, "Good people attract good people, so why not ask for good people? You don't want referrals to people who are egomaniacs, control freaks, or verbally rude and abusive—life is too short."

7. Ask your contact to give you three or four referrals, not "a laundry list." Then get as much information about those three or four individuals as you can. The more you find out, the more productive your contacts will be when you actually reach them.

Eighty percent of people have what Bruso calls the Target return syndrome. When you return goods to a Target store, you take a number and wait in a long line, which is how many people work when they attempt to grow their businesses. However, when you follow the Power Referral Program, you go straight to the front of the line. And when you make your connection, your contact knows that someone close to him or her feels that you are trustworthy, likable, and competent and have integrity.

The referral expert Joanne Black has a similar approach. She advises clients to make a list of 100 people they know and then organize it by putting those they know best at the top regardless who they are or what they do. Start at the top, meet with them, and say, "I have a new strategy for my business. I would like to bounce it off you and get your feedback."

The purpose of the meeting is to get feedback, not referrals. Be very precise about who you wish to meet. Don't ask these people for their business. Instead, ask them who they know. Work your way down the list. The more you do and the more you ask, the more momentum will build, and you may have problems pursuing all the leads you get.

Most people are happy to make referrals. Joanne Black worked with an outplacement firm that surveyed 50 of its top clients. On the last part of this four-phase survey, Black inserted the question, "Would you be willing to make a referral to this company?" On a 7-point scale, with 7 being the highest, the responses averaged 6.5.

Referral Arrangements

If your business is going to involve referrals, clarify whether money or other compensation will be exchanged. Few things can destroy a relationship faster than misunderstandings and bruised feelings relating to referral fees. Specifically ask your referral partners if they are willing to give and expect to receive referral fees. If referral fees will be paid, clarify the amounts and how and when they will be paid.

Referral fees are always negotiable; my normal practice is to offer my referral sources 10 percent of what I receive on all fees over $500. Under that amount, it doesn't pay. Since referral arrangements are supposed to be reciprocal, I also clarify to my referral partners that I expect to receive 10 percent of the fees they receive from customers or clients I recommend. With businesses in which the profit margin is not high, I will accept a 5 percent referral fee.

When a source and I reach agreement on referral fee terms, I send him or her a confirming e-mail that restates the terms. On every subsequent referral to or from that source, I also send an e-mail that states the client's name, thanks him or her for giving or taking the referral, and confirming the referral fee terms.

Regardless of the amount, always agree on the arrangement up front. It can save you lots of aggravation and bitter feelings.

Since referral fee amounts can differ, I keep track of all referral arrangements on my contact software and note them in my client files. My software has a line item for commissions, so I enter the

---

Research before you recommend. The first people I recommend are those I have worked with because I can attest to the quality of their work. Nothing is better than a referral that says, "That's who I use. I think he's the best."

When I make a referral, I point out any problems I know of. I disclose that the person tends to run late or is slow returning mail and calls. When I receive referrals, I ask the source to fill me in on any problems he or she knows.

agreed amount of the referral fee on that line. I also check off on my software that I sent an e-mail confirming the referral fee terms.

Giving referrals and receiving referrals often go hand in hand, so give the level of referrals you wish to receive. Don't make referrals unless you're sure that those you recommend can deliver. If people I don't know well ask me for referrals, I try to meet with them to see how they present and handle themselves. I ask them to tell me about themselves, what they do, how they work, and who they serve. Then I request that they send me information about themselves and check their Internet presence; if they have a Web site, I check out what it looks like and anything else I can find.

■ ■ ■ **CONNECTING LINK** ■ ■ ■

When you make referrals, zero in on the fit. Connect those who would make the best match. For example, I know many writers, but they specialize in different areas. They are editors, proofreaders, indexers, copywriters, publicists, journalists, feature writers, screenwriters, ghostwriters, historians, and novelists. When someone needs a press release written, I'm not going to recommend a historian.

Be wary of those who claim, "I can do everything." They can't! They also can't do everything well. If a copywriter claims that she can write great press releases, be cautious. In most cases, she or he will not write it as well as those who specialize in that type of writing.

Find out people's specialties. Avoid Jacks- or Jills-of-all-trades because it's virtually impossible for them to do everything excellently. If you want excellence, which you should, find a specialist who comes highly recommended. Yes, you'll have to pay a premium, a higher price, but in most cases it will be money well spent. Usually you get better, more professional service from specialists.

Specialists also can contribute more. Since they do a particular kind of work all the time, they usually know all the ins and outs. Most of them know shortcuts and best practices that can save you time and money. They usually know what would work best for you and are up on important new trends and developments.

Specialists are more likely to give you what you want or need. When you need your office painted, you may think immediately of the graphic designer who created your letterhead because she had such a brilliant color sense. However, she probably doesn't know about the unique new shades of exterior latex that just hit the market or which painters would be best for your job.

> "All our business comes from referrals," says Steve Lillo, CEO of the Web site design firm PlanetLink (www.planetlink.com). "Some of our clients regularly refer new projects to us, so in appreciation, we give them special rates. It works out great for all of us because PlanetLink gets a steady stream of new referrals and my clients get a discount and know that the people they refer to us are in good hands."

Before I make a referral, I ask for references and call to verify them. References can have limited value, however, because of the following issues:

- People usually won't supply the names of people who won't give them rave reviews. Depend on your intuition and read between the lines. Follow your instincts; if anything said or unsaid causes you to react, follow up and probe more deeply.
- Individuals who worked well with one person may not be right for you. It could be because of their ability, personality, or a million other factors, including what is going on at that time in their lives. At best, relying on references is a gamble, so listen to your instincts, which are usually more dependable. We all have to take risks, and some don't work out.
- Getting certain referrals may not be advisable for you. In your desire to do business, you may be tempted to hook

up with people you should avoid. Working with them could set you back by forcing you to work on tasks you have grown beyond. Certain clients or work could conflict with or cost you other clients, not give you enough money, or hamper you career in other ways.

Sometimes you can sense that a potential client will be difficult. Your referral source may warn you or you may hear rumors through the grapevine. A prospect may sound abrupt, cold, or confused. He or she could be difficult to reach, a poor communicator, particular, demanding, tight with money, or impossible to please.

When I evaluate whether to work with a prospective client, I always measure the aggravation factor. I ask myself, "Is this a project I should avoid because this person or job will give me too much stress and aggravation?" If that is the case, I don't take it. If I'm not sure whether to work on a project, I jack my price way up. I try to price myself out of the job, and that usually scares the prospect away.

■ ■ ■ Premarketing

Have referral sources premarket you. This means that when they recommend you, they should sell you to potential clients and make them eager to work with you. Then, when potential clients contact you, all you have to do is close the deal—if you want to work with them.

Most referral sources will premarket you if they know you produce outstanding results. Most sources want to recommend only the best because it makes them look good and they prefer to associate with the best.

I have reciprocal arrangements with people all over North America. When I'm scheduled to speak or give my crash course in their areas, I send them my flyers announcing the events. They then e-mail my material to their clients and contacts along with a personal note. Often the note will read, "Exiting news! Jill will be in town on November 15 to present her fabulous crash course on publicity, which you should not miss. If you sign up by October 15, here's a special price for you."

Here are a few things you should do when you are thinking about referrals:

- Help your referral sources recommend ideal clients to you by giving them the profile of your ideal client. Explain the type of business you want and the kinds of individuals with whom you wish to work. If you have brochures, handouts, or other materials describing your business and the benefits it provides, send them to your referral sources. Then they can prescreen prospects for you.
- Keep your referral sources advised. When you agree to work with a referred client, notify the source. As you work with that client, periodically keep the referral source up to date. By staying in contact with your referral source, you could exchange information that might prove helpful to each of you.

All business involves risk, and the smartest business operators buy goods and services on the basis of risk, not price. They purchase that which will put them at the least risk. In addition, they will pay a premium because those goods and services have a better chance of working. Risk and trust are tied inexorably together.

Action Plan

1. In creating networks, list at least three types of experts or specialists with whom you should align yourself.

   _____

   _____

   _____

2. Define your three most important core values.

   _____

   _____

   _____

3. State how you will keep track of all your referral arrangements.

   _____

   _____

   _____

   _____

4. List 10 people you can meet with to begin the Power Referral Program.

   _____

   _____

   _____

   _____

   _____

   _____

   _____

   _____

   _____

4

Myths and Misconceptions

We all have misconceptions about business. Some of them are myths that have been perpetuated by the use of traditional approaches that no longer work; others are theories that may have sounded good once but never made sense. Getting noticed is no exception.

The following are myths and misconceptions that people still believe about self-promotion. Try not to fall into the trap of following them. Myths and misconceptions in this area include the following:

1. All publicity is good publicity.

   MYTH: *If people recognize your name for any reason, that is beneficial. Traditional wisdom was that consumers had short memories and would be drawn to those with familiar names no matter what they were famous for.*

   REALITY: Times have changed, competition is fierce, and quality is now the primary objective. People want results. Although they may enjoy superficial contact with celebrities or be mesmerized by designer labels, they ultimately want value. They don't want to do business with crooks, rogues, and incompetents—except those who enjoy throwing money away. Bad publicity will come back to haunt you.

2. If it's not broken, don't fix it.

   MYTH: *Don't tinker with a successful formula. In the past, business operators could afford to be cautious and rest on their laurels. People loved to do business with well-established "name" firms. When those companies found the right formula, they stayed with it and didn't stray. The rationale they gave was the New Coke disaster, when Coca Cola changed its recipe and nearly destroyed its legendary brand.*

   REALITY: In business today you can't stand still; you must move forward and improve constantly. If you do not, the competition will steal your market. To survive, today's businesses must examine their operations continuously to find how they can be improved. Study your market and other markets; learn about trends, developments, and emerging companies; see what the competition is doing and how it could affect your business. Constantly see how you can improve.

3. This is the story.

   MYTH: *When we tell our story, we assume that the facts are the facts and everyone will get them right. Since we know what occurred, we believe that our version is the version that will be told.*

   REALITY: As soon as your story is out, it no longer belongs to you. Kate Adamson's appearance on the *O'Reilly Factor* generated a huge response but ended up telling the wrong story. Kate and her husband, Steven Klugman, did everything they could to get the facts across, including talking to the program's fact checkers and screeners. Despite their efforts, O'Reilly assumed that Kate had been in a coma, which she had not. Therefore, he asked Kate questions that she couldn't answer because they didn't relate to what she actually had experienced. As a result, the story that most of the media covered and that most people came to believe was based on the mistakes O'Reilly made. Now O'Reilly's version is the account that is repeated and has become attached to Kate.

■ ■ ■ **CONNECTING LINK** ■ ■ ■

When people get major facts wrong, immediately correct them. Politely but clearly and firmly set the record straight. Otherwise your story could be co-opted and distorted, which can be harmful or at least do you no good.

4. Just because I have a great product, I'll succeed.

MYTH: *Many people have the erroneous impression that when they have a good product or service, all they have to do is put out a sign and get a phone listing and customers will flock to them. These misguided people may have fabulous credentials, unequaled experience, and talent galore. They may do brilliant work. However, none of that means they will attract lots of customers.*

REALITY: "The entrepreneurial graveyard is filled with business owners who had good products and services," Mark LeBlanc observes. To succeed, you must promote your goods or services actively; your target audience must know that you're in business and how you can help them. Delivering that message is essential if you hope to survive. Simply put, you must get the right clients and customers: those who need what you offer. In business, being the "best-kept secret" does not translate into great success. How successful is the chiropractor with no patients?

5. People will find me. I will get what I deserve.

   MYTH: *Many people think that if they open a business, hang up a shingle, or put up a sign, customers will appear magically. They feel that because they worked so hard to become experts, their hard work automatically will be rewarded and they will become highly successful. They expect their just desserts.*

   REALITY: I believe in Karma, but some people ask too much. Doing the work to become qualified is just part of the job. Once you're qualified, you must continue to work hard. As I've stressed, competition is brutal; battles over the same clients are fought constantly. It's arrogant to think that you can just sit back and wait to be discovered; it also makes no sense.

6. I can run my entire business.

   MYTH: *Business is extremely complex. A physician may be a medical expert but know little about business management, patient retention, advertising, scheduling appointments, insurance claims, or even keeping books. Yet a physician may try to take on these tasks until he or she is forced to get help.*

   REALITY: We can't do everything; business has become entirely too involved. Keeping most accounts and filing taxes usually is best left to specialists and may not be where your time and effort should be spent. Even if you know how to run your business, you probably will not be as efficient as a business management specialist. Hire the best people you can afford; they will lighten your load and usually do a better job. They also could be a source of referrals that could more than compensate for their cost. Build a team and remember that you don't have to build it all at once.

7. Hit them hard and fast.

   MYTH: *People are taught that at meetings they should establish that they're important and demonstrate their expertise quickly, and so they try to make a strong impression immediately by grabbing the spotlight and firing away. They frequently participate too soon and become too involved. After the initial flurry, they often have little to say.*

   REALITY: Sitting quietly, letting others speak, and listening are usually more effective than firing first and flaring out. Melt into the background, listen, observe, and wait. Fully understand all that is being said, all the implications, and then contribute. Generally, it will give you a better grasp and help you be more influential.

8. Bowl them over.

   MYTH: *More is not always more. Many people think that they have to impress others by demonstrating how much they know. Therefore, they frequently go overboard and swamp people with useless knowledge. Many lecturers get so lost in details that they don't realize that they're putting their audiences to sleep.*

   REALITY: Too much information is unnecessary and can work against you. It can confuse people and cause them to lose interest. Editing is an art, and less is frequently more. People who give too much information tend to talk at people, not to them. Giving people less information can force them to ask questions, get help, and find experts who can fill in their gaps.

9. Sources will not share.

   MYTH: *When you ask for information about a person you would like to meet, your sources won't be forthcoming. People are reluctant to share information and their sources.*

REALITY: When people have dealt with you, trust you, like you, and believe in you, they will give you tons of information. They will trust you and share their confidences. They will want you to succeed. If they are convinced that you will do a great job for their contacts, they will make your job easier because you will make them look good as well.

10. You could be helping them.

    MYTH: *When you ask for referrals, you are asking for favors. Many people have been taught not to request favors; some feel it's impolite, and others don't want to become obligated.*

    REALITY: When you ask for referrals, you are giving your contact the opportunity to help his or her friends. If you perform excellently and provide value, your contacts will be delighted to recommend you because their recommendation will benefit their friends greatly. Learn to ask for and give help graciously; it's how life works best.

11. Successful people don't ask.

    MYTH: *When people ask for referrals, that is a sign of weakness because it means that their business isn't doing well.*

    REALITY: Look at the most successful people you know. You will find that the bulk, if not all, of their business comes from referrals. Referrals are how they built their businesses, and they continue to cultivate referrals to maintain and develop it.

12. Request a referral, not an introduction.

    MYTH: *If I get a name, it's a referral. Therefore, my sources only have to provide me with names and nothing more.*

REALITY: Joanne Black emphasizes that if a person doesn't know you, it's still a cold call. You need something more than a contact's name. You must get an introduction from your referral source. He or she must make a phone call, send an e-mail, or show up personally for a meeting or lunch.

13. The media want news.

    MYTH: *Publicity is hard to get. The media are interested only in the biggest stars and celebrities and have no interest in you.*

    REALITY: If your story is news, the media want and need you. News is the media's lifeblood; it's how the media exist. Without stories, newspapers would be empty and the airways would be silent. If you have news for the media, the media not only want you, they will pursue you. Take your story and make it newsworthy.

14. Stories don't have long tails.

    MYTH: *When a story about you appears, that's the best day because you get the maximum coverage. From then on, it's all downhill.*

    REALITY: Coverage of you can have a long life if you preserve it. Get copies of stories about you or of your appearances. Obtain transcripts of programs or your interviews. Post them on your Web site, distribute them in mailings and handouts, and attach them to your résumé. Sprinkle excerpts and quotes throughout your promotional materials. Ultimately, they can bring you more publicity and more business than you received from the original coverage.

Action Plan

1. Give three examples of publicity that was not good publicity.

_____

_____

_____

_____

2. List three or four tasks that you could use expert help in performing.

_____

_____

_____

_____

_____

3. If you believe that you're too busy, list three tasks that you could not do or assign to others.

_____

_____

_____

_____

4. What other myths have you heard about publicity that may not be true?

_____

_____

_____

_____

_____

_____

5

Why Are You Knocking Yourself Out?

This chapter will cover:

- Writing a wish list
- Recognizing that passion motivates
- Taking stock
- Enlisting help
- Advocate lists

WHAT DO YOU WANT from life? What would you like to do? How do you wish to be remembered? Is the way you do business helping you reach those goals? Examine your values, determine what is most important to you, and then distinguish yourself by being true to your values.

When you're true to your values, people notice; they admire and respect you. From your behavior, they can tell that your values extend to every aspect of your life, including your business. When they respect you for adhering to your values, they will trust you and be more prone to do business with you.

Working to further your values also fires your passion and gives you a greater incentive to succeed. People respond to your passion; they buy into your values and offer their support. When they sign on and work with you, everything becomes easier, more exciting, and more worthwhile and tends to be more successful.

Identify your values; get a clear understanding of what is most important to you. Since your values will affect the way you direct your life, make sure that you are being true to them and continuously moving along the right path. If you see that you have strayed, make whatever adjustments are necessary.

■ ■ ■ **CONNECTING LINK** ■ ■ ■

My primary values are being honest, helping others, and doing the best I possibly can. Kindness is also important to me; I want it to permeate my life. I try to be kind to others and hope they will be pleasant to me. I understand that pressure can cause people to act brusquely, rudely, even harshly. When they do, I try not to respond on the same level. I demand more of myself; I insist on being true to my values regardless of how difficult that may be.

Examine your values. Take a close look at them in the context of your business. Ask yourself the following questions:

- What do I want from my work?
- Who would I like to work with?
- What kind of people are they?
- What tasks would I rather not do?
- Which people do I wish to avoid?

It's your life, so chart it in the direction you choose. At certain points, especially when you're getting started, it may be hard because you may not think you have many options. It may seem that you have few interesting job opportunities or little chance of advancement. Even then—especially then—stay true to your values.

Dig in, stand firm, and perform at the highest levels. Don't be a victim of the wishes or behavior of others; set your own course and stick to it.

Remain flexible. Expect obstacles and hurdles. Understand that some targets may simply not be reachable, at least at this time. You may have to adjust your approach, go to plan B, connect with the second person on your list, or wait. Tell everyone what you want because you never know who could help. They might give you critical information or introduce you to people who can help you reach your goals.

■ ■ ■ Writing a Wish List

To clarify what you want, try this exercise: Write a list of at least 10 things that you would like your business to provide for you. Be totally honest; don't hold back but list anything that would fulfill your dreams. Don't be influenced by what you believe others would think, whether they would approve or disapprove, or whether any of your wishes are realistic. List what you truly want, items that could affect other aspects of your life, and don't be afraid to be fanciful.

Take your time; don't rush. Write the list over the course of a few days, weeks, or even months. Go at your own pace. This exercise is not a race, and no one is keeping score except you. The main requirement is that you list what *you* most deeply want; the main objective is to learn about yourself.

Many people pursue goals that are set by others rather than seeking what they actually want. They listen to and are influenced by parents and teachers. They adopt their suggestions and suppress their own dreams. Margaret became an engineer because her parents and teachers complimented her preciseness, deductive reasoning, and skill at math. They took special pride in Margaret's accomplishments because no one else in the family exhibited similar skills. Margaret enjoyed their praise and worked hard for it. When it came time to select her career, she deferred to their influence despite the fact that her lifelong dream was to design high-fashion clothing.

We choose vocations for a variety of reasons: to make money, be of service, continue a family tradition, lead a certain type of life, or please our parents, teachers, or society. Deciding to become a dentist may have paved the way to a scholarship or to being accepted by a particular school. Or it might have been done solely to impress some little cutie. It may have been done to fulfill Dad's shattered dream.

It's your life. Be true to yourself. Follow *your* dreams.

Recognizing That Passion Motivates

Deferring to others may seem to be the "most sensible" route, especially if you're young and impressionable and think you have few options. However, it can extract an enormous price. Not following your passions can mute your voice. You won't be as inspired or do your work as well. It can give you a miserable life. What could be worse than spending every day doing what you don't like? But millions of people do that, and many of them become bitter. Frequently, those feelings sabotage or limit the extent of their success.

Unhappiness can be infectious. It tends to spill over into your personal life and sap happiness from your loved ones' lives. Your decision to work at a job you hate sets a terrible example for your family, one that they may end up following.

In contrast, passion is an unparalleled motivator. It can whisk you past obstacles in nothing flat and make those experiences exciting, rewarding, and fun. When you follow your passions, it's not work; it's a breeze. Your curiosity and enthusiasm drive you, make you hungry to learn and understand everything about your interest. You connect with kindred spirits, people with similar passions; you learn together, teach, grow, and become experts together. Together you make breakthroughs that help others and advance your field and the state of the art.

Passion enables you to get noticed. People respond to your fire and want to be within its glow. They tell others and spread your message and your acclaim. They support your efforts and help you succeed.

I will discuss passion at length in Chapter 10.

■ ■ ■ Taking Stock

Define yourself so that when you approach others, they will understand precisely what you do and the benefits you can provide. If you can't define yourself clearly, other people won't be able to send you good referrals because they won't understand what you do and can provide. They won't be able to tell others about you if they don't understand what you do.

"The most important requirement to get noticed is articulation," Mark LeBlanc believes. "Articulation is everything. If you can't articulate who you are and what you do, you are dead in the water because all prospects have a smell test. You need more than a sound bite; you need to be able to answer the five critical questions [see below] that people will ask, and 90 percent of those in business can't."

People who cannot articulate tend to hold back; they usually don't put themselves out there, LeBlanc notes. "They won't pick up the phone, go to a networking meeting, talk to someone, or go out of their way to meet or speak with others. They fear that they will be asked questions that they can't answer, which will make them look bad."

The ability to define oneself is the most essential marketing tool. LeBlanc says that to define yourself, you must answer the following questions and clearly express the answers:

1. Who are you? What are your experience and qualifications? Why should people listen to you and take you seriously?
2. What do you do? What can you bring to the table that will persuade people to do business with you and/or recommend you?
3. How do you do it? How is your process different from that of others, and what makes it better?
4. What precise benefits do you provide? Why should prospects work with or buy from you? What's in it for them? Are you just trading on your reputation, background, experience, contacts, or friends?

5. How much do you charge? Does it make financial sense for prospects to consider you? Will purchasing your goods or services be a good investment?

Most people don't assess themselves accurately; they can't see their actual strengths and weaknesses objectively. They may fall short in areas in which they think they shine and miss talents that others clearly see.

To assess your strengths and weaknesses more accurately, ask your friends, family, and business associates to do the following:

- Describe the areas in which you excel
- Explain why they like dealing with you
- Identify the areas that could be improved

You probably will be surprised by their comments, but don't ignore them because they probably will be spot-on.

Decide what you want to achieve. An example of goals could be meeting an expert who can give you great referrals, receiving strong sales leads, or getting access to new breakthrough products. Once you know what you want, create a plan. Determine where you are now and chart a course to your objective.

Build on your strengths to find the best and shortest route to get from where you are to where you wish to be. Then break the journey into smaller intermediate steps. List all the milestones that must be met at every stage, all the work you must complete.

If you're trying to connect with particular individuals, determine the following:

1. Who you want to approach.
2 The order in which you should contact them.
3. The questions you should ask them and the requests you should make.
4. How long you expect it to take; then add some more time to your estimate.

Chart alternative routes. Decide which approach would be the quickest and easiest to achieve and the most productive. Could any of your options enable you to reap other benefits along the way that might make your time better spent?

When you select your targets, explore cross-promotional opportunities. If you are a weight-loss expert, explain your services to physicians, psychologists, diet-product sellers, fitness clubs, personal trainers, and women's organizations. Post flyers in bakeries, ice cream parlors, and candy stores. Find people who regularly deal with your target audience and can recommend your services.

Recently, I met with a financial planner who asked me, "Who is your CPA and do you mind if I contact him?" I told her, and soon thereafter the planner called my CPA, said that I had given her his name, and scheduled an appointment.

At their appointment, the planner explained to my CPA who she was, described her background, and laid out the types of services she could provide for my CPA's clients. My CPA was impressed with the planner's focus and qualifications and has referred a number of his clients to her.

Instead of trying to market herself directly to people who might need her services, the planner targeted CPAs because they could give her credibility with a large referral pool. Her plan was to build her business by leveraging the trust relationships that CPAs have built with their clients. Although not all the CPAs the planner contacted provided referrals, enough did to enable her to increase her business significantly.

To find people who are trusted by and can introduce you to the type of clients or customers you seek, take the following steps:

- Identify your target market and the services those people use.

- Which of those service providers could be big referral sources for you?
- Make a list and prioritize it into A, B, and C groups, the order in which you want to contact them.

Start at the top of the pyramid with your A list. First, try to reach potential referral sources that could send you the most or the highest-quality business.

The top players are usually hard, if not impossible, to reach. Many of them have gatekeepers who, as part of their duties, concentrate on turning away people such as you. Frequently, the only way to get past a gatekeeper is through an introduction by someone connected to his or her boss.

If you can't connect with your top targets, systematically work your way down your lists. After you've gone through all names on the A list, start contacting everyone on the B and C lists. Try to spot up-and-comers who could develop into outstanding referral sources. Grow with your referral sources; build strong bonds and mutually beneficial long-term relationships with them.

When you speak with your targets, be precise. Explain exactly how you can serve them and their clients. Remember that they will be focused on results and will be going out on a limb to recommend

■ ■ ■ **CONNECTING LINK** ■ ■ ■

Don't form referral alliances unless you're an expert in your field. Avoid plunging into water over your head. Know your subject cold, inside out. Make sure that you can answer every question and deliver what they need. Have your friends and associates question and test you.

When a contact asks a question that you cannot answer, don't bluff. Say, "I'm not sure about the answer, but let me check on it and I'll get back to you soon." Then, as soon as possible, find the answer and tell your contact.

you. Tell your targets how you can save their clients money on taxes and provide lower-cost products, faster and more expert installation, training, longer-lasting products, better customer service, top technical assistance, and business referrals.

■ ■ ■ Enlisting Help

A number of my clients write monthly e-mail newsletters; that is a great way to reach many people fast. Newsletters provide great publicity, position you as an expert, and keep you on people's radar screens. Although not everyone can put out a monthly newsletter, anyone can hire people who can do that.

Don't get stuck on "I can't do this." Get help. Find people who can perform important tasks for you and hire them. And remember that the people you hire will be a potential source of referrals to you if you treat them well.

Enlist help from people in your industry, even those who might be your competitors. They may have too much work or jobs they don't want or lack the time to take on. Therefore, they may recommend you.

Melodye, an aptly named harpist, performed regularly at small local events but couldn't get higher-profile engagements. Finally, she was offered a larger booking, and she called a busy, well-established violinist to ask how much he charged for giving similar performances. After he explained his fees, Melodye mentioned that she was looking for work and asked if he or his contacts ever needed a harpist. Shortly thereafter, he began to refer business to her and recommended her for a number of larger engagements. In the process, Melodye learned that she was charging too little for her services and was able to raise her price.

Don't be bashful. Let people know what you can provide, that you're available, and how they can help. Send out your soldiers.

Don't let pride stop you. Some people think that asking for help tells others that they're not busy or not doing well. If you think this way, observe successful people who have built their businesses through referrals. They are still asking for referrals and doing what helped get them to the top.

When you ask for referrals, describe your ideal client or customer. Be specific. The more specific you are, the easier it will be for your source to identify the best candidates for you. Tell your sources exactly what you want because if they don't know, they can't help you.

"Be an artist: The more color and lines you include in the painting, the easier it will be for people to see what it means," Joanne Black stresses. Educate your referral sources about who exactly you are looking for and then ask them to introduce you.

WARNING ▶ Never say, "Do you know anyone who could use my services?" Start by explaining that you are seeking referrals and specifically identify who you would like to meet. Ask, "Do you know anyone who needs a top inventory accountant, a business travel agent, or a patent attorney?"

You may have to work in increments and go through three or four intermediary contacts before connecting with your ultimate target. When multiple steps are involved, more research, planning, and patience are usually necessary.

When you ask for help, show your appreciation; don't be cheap or small-minded or have tunnel vision. "A woman asked me to lunch to pick my brain, which I was happy to do," Mimi Donaldson reports. "We went to a Japanese noodle house and spoke well into the afternoon. When the check arrived, it was less than $15, but instead of footing the bill, she examined it, made some calculations, and told me my share. I looked at her like she was crazy. I gave her my half, but I never returned any of her calls. I certainly didn't want to have any further contact, much less help, with someone who was so ungrateful, tight, and small-minded."

■ ■ ■ Advocate Lists

Mark LeBlanc has developed the Target-25 Strategy for helping his clients get referrals. Here's how his strategy works.

Identify the 25 most important people in your life who are in a position to affect your business. They constitute your advocate list. Then contact each of them every month to create "top of mind" presence that reminds them of you and what you do.

Each month, send or do something tiny and don't ask for referrals. The objective of this strategy is to stay on each list member's radar. One month, send a copy of your newsletter and then forward an interesting article. Alternate between calling by telephone and sending holiday cards, a cartoon, a business or life tip, or an article.

You can phone, fax, mail, e-mail, or visit list members. When I trained at the American embassy in China, I sent each member of my advocate list a beautiful postcard. I have also sent "Thanks a Million" chocolate bars, announcements of significant events such as the publication of one of my books or a major speaking engagement, and personal handwritten notes.

I think handwritten cards and notes add a personal touch. Although my objective is to remind people that I'm still out there and am doing interesting things, I think that handwritten notes set the warm, personal tone I want to establish and maintain in my relationships.

LeBlanc suggests writing an article, photocopying it, and sending a copy to each member of your advocate list. Attach a note to each saying, "Hi, Jim. I hope all is well. I thought you might like this article that I wrote. Feel free to send it to your friends, colleagues, or clients who it could help."

Don't ask for referrals. "The essence of the strategy is neutrality," LeBlanc explains. "You are not asking or depending on them for anything. All you're doing is remaining on the top of their minds, re-minding them of you and whatever it is that you do."

Regardless of how much they like and believe in you, your advocates are busy. They have so much going on that you will slip to the back of their minds if you don't send them little nudges. When you stay in monthly contact, you remain at the top of their minds and receive more referrals.

LeBlanc spends no more than $50 and typically from one to four hours per month on his strategy. He reviews his advocate list yearly but suggests that if you're new in business, you should review it as often as every 90 days. Then, as your business grows, a yearly review will suffice.

To keep you advocate list strong, don't expand it beyond 25 members or dilute it with friends or weaker connections. A larger, more extensive list can be unwieldy and difficult to manage.

I have strayed from LeBlanc's formula by adding people whom I have not met but want to target for my advocate list. I don't contact only those I've already connected with; I also contact those with whom I want to be connected.

In addition, I maintain an alliance list, which is a notch below my advocate list. I contact those on my alliance list every quarter to keep myself on their radar. They are friends, associates, and business contacts, and I've worked and partnered with most of them. However, they are not my champions or true advocates as those on my advocate list are.

Action Plan

1. List at least 10 things that you would like to achieve or obtain from building a network of referrals.

_____

_____

_____

_____

_____

_____

_____

_____

_____

2. Define yourself so that other people can make good referrals to you.

_____

_____

_____

3. Who would you include on your advocate and alliance lists?

_____

_____

_____

_____

4. List six items that you could send the members of your advocate list.

_____

_____

_____

_____

_____

_____

6

Where To Get Noticed

This chapter will cover:

- Getting into the game
- Organizations
- Local groups
- Industry groups
- Structured groups
- Referral and resource groups
- Starting your own group

NOW THAT YOU HAVE clarified why you want to get noticed, it's time to take action. For many people, getting started, taking that first step, is impossible; it paralyzes them. The best-selling author and speaker T. Harv Eker has the ideal advice for these people: "Ready, fire, aim." He believes that it's better to shoot from the hip than never to fire.

In whatever you do, take that first essential step: Dive into the water. You may have developed the ideal solution for a major problem or invented a product that fills a critical void, but what good are they if you never implement your plans? Don't waste your time sitting around thinking, planning, and tinkering because you will never get your businesses off the ground that way. Instead, get started, do something, make a move. Put yourself out there and see where you land. Get wet—soaking wet.

Many people have little or no business experience. They have never taken business courses and don't understand business terms. Business scares them; it's alien territory, a place where they feel they don't belong. When it comes to business, they don't know what to do, where to turn, or who to ask for help. They are completely lost. They want to go into business but fear that they will be devoured. Before long, the fire that fueled their passion sputters and dies.

But you can't succeed without trying. Venturing out and taking chances is the only way to learn and to succeed. Many people simply won't try because they are afraid to fail. They don't try because it's easier for their fragile psyches to accept that they didn't try than to admit that they tried and failed. They would rather not try than try and not succeed.

■ ■ ■ Getting into the Game

To me, standing around spinning my wheels and watching others pass me by is not living life; it's missing life. It's staying on the sidelines and watching others play the game.

I love the game: the excitement, the learning, meeting and building relationships with new and different people. People fascinate me, and their stories amaze me. Frequently I want to pinch myself because I work with and meet an astonishing array of outstanding people who constantly contribute wonders to my life.

I prefer to be active and busy and expose myself to stimulating new people and experiences. This exposure has introduced me to amazing opportunities, remarkable individuals, and interests that have changed my life. It also has introduced me to talents, parts of myself that I never knew I possessed. It has enabled me to continue to grow and enjoy a rich, productive life.

Identify new areas and people who could inject excitement into your business and your life. Investigate new topics; learn about and explore them. See how they could expand your business and help you perform better.

Occasionally, we all get stuck. At one time or another most of us have had a daunting paper to write and have waited until the last possible moment. We did everything to avoid the task until our only choice was to start writing or flunk. Finally, in total fear, we sat down to write. The first few words were agony. They might even have drawn blood. The initial paragraph had the grace of an armored tank and moved just as fast. But then we found the rhythm, words broke loose, and sentences formed. Ideas emerged, the momentum grew, and we got into a flow. Suddenly, we were immersed in our writing, were lost in our thoughts, and were expressing them clearly, directly, and logically—to our utter surprise.

How many people do you know who have the careers they initially planned or began with? I know very few. Years ago people chose a business or career and stayed in it for life, but today that's not the norm. People develop new interests, evolve, and change careers. Some move from career to career and then back again. And experts predict that this practice will increase.

The most interesting and successful individuals I know have ended up in careers vastly different from those with which they began. Somewhere in their trajectory, they came across an interesting subject, person, insight, experience, or opportunity. Their contacts, curiosity, or knowledge carried them into the unknown, where they met kindred spirits who helped them along the way.

I went to school to study psychology and never thought about publicity. Before Jay Conrad Levinson became the world's best-selling business writer, he had a career in advertising. Speaker of the U.S. House of Representatives Nancy Pelosi was a housewife who didn't run for public office until her children were grown.

What you're doing may be great, but something better, more lucrative, or more fulfilling could be just around the corner. Continue what you're doing but be alert to new challenges and opportunities. Probe, explore, and put yourself in positions where you can meet and be noticed by people who can help you become happier and more successful.

■ ■ ■ Organizations

Now that you know that you have to take action and begin, where do you start? Consider organizational events. They can be the ideal places to begin making contacts because virtually everyone who attends these events is there to network and make connections. Frequently, these events are structured to facilitate networking. Specific times have been set aside for the attendees to meet one another, interact, and connect.

The fact that these events are networking-oriented can take the pressure off shy, uncomfortable newcomers. Since everybody has the same agenda—to connect with others—strangers frequently will approach you, introduce themselves, and engage you in conversations. When you talk with others, it breaks the tension and makes it less frightening. You find that talking to the next person is easier and that you're more comfortable.

A dizzying number of organizations hold networking events, so the trick is to attend those which could be most productive for you. Choosing the best events can take a little investigation, and although every group is a potential source of referrals, some are clearly better than others. Therefore, it is usually worth the time and effort to learn which can be the most beneficial for you. Or you could start your own group.

Groups serve different audiences and have different slants or purposes. Civic organizations support community projects, women's groups work to promote women's causes, and industry associations serve the members of their particular fields. I always belong to a number of groups.

Before you join organizations, make sure to do the following:

- Clarify your objectives for both the short term and the long term. List what you want to accomplish and how long you think it will take.
- Precisely identify your target audience. Know exactly who you want to meet: travel writers, classic car restorers, or wine distributors. Then go to organizational events that they would attend.
- In identifying your targets, look for cross-promotional opportunities. Members of certain groups may not use your goods or services themselves but could give you entry to a large number of people who will.
- Learn about each organization; investigate what you may be getting into. Ask about its mission, agenda, membership profile, events, and causes; how often it meets; and the commitment you will be expected to make. If you're young and new in business, do you want to join an established service organization that has an older demographic? Perhaps you do in order to meet key players in your field.
- Speak with your friends and business associates. Learn about their experiences and what they would recommend for you. Be their guest at meetings and events and experience them for yourself.
- Before you join an organization, speak with at least one member. Get a general overview of the group, its strong points, what it's like to belong, how it could help you, and information about its members. Specifically ask what they like best and least. Usually, those you speak with will introduce you at your first meeting or even sponsor you, which will help you make contacts and gain credibility.

Join organizations in your field but also venture out. If you're a publicist, join publicity associations but also think about going to au-

Most organizations will let you attend one or two meetings or events before requiring you to join. Go to their meetings and try them out. See if you like the organization and its members and want to join.

Some organizations operate casually. When you become a member, they don't require you to attend meetings and events regularly but will let you drop in occasionally. Find out about each organization's policy before you join.

Don't expect immediate results. Usually, organization members want to get to know more about you before they refer business to you. Be patient and get greater visibility, recognition, and trust. Don't be discouraged if an organization doesn't provide referrals for you immediately.

thors groups because writers need publicity. If you're the only insurance salesperson who belongs to the motorcycle club, it could help you sell policies. Joining organizations outside your own industry also can turn you on to new and fascinating people and interests, which can stimulate and add excitement to your life.

■ ■ CONNECTING LINK ■ ■

Don't rule out groups that have nothing to do with business, such as those which are charitable, religious, athletic, social, or hobby-oriented. Members of these organizations are usually happy to recommend people they like who share their interests. Attending organizational events where you can have fun, help others, and work for causes that reflect your values can be good business and very fulfilling. Remember that having fun with others is a marvelous bonding experience.

When you join organizations, decide how involved you want to be. Devoting your time to causes, serving on committees, and being an officer can increase your profile dramatically. Ask yourself if you can afford the time, effort, or expense of leading a campaign or being a director. Is it worthwhile for you? Or will your service be rewarding enough to justify the time?

▪ ▪ ▪ Local Groups

No matter how far you branch out or how successful you become, it's essential to remain closely connected to your local community: your Chamber of Commerce and business, civic, and community groups. These organizations will be your base; their members will be the core advocates who will root for you, support you, and spread your fame. When you try to expand beyond your local area, they can give strong endorsements when people in the new markets ask about you.

Build local visibility and trust. Your reputation will grow when the members who live in your community recognize that you consistently perform excellently. You will have gained their trust. Trust is essential in getting referrals. To recommend you, top businesspeople, the referral sources you want, must be convinced that you will perform excellently. If they don't trust you, they will not send you business because your failure will reflect negatively on them. However, if these individuals see you, know you, and are aware of your reputation, trusting that you will perform well is not a giant leap. When given the opportunity, they usually will refer business to you.

When you're active in local organizations, you contribute to the areas where you live, work, and have strong personal ties. You support the causes and values in which you believe. Being connected to your roots helps you learn what is happening in your community. It enables you to understand the economic, political, and social climate. It keeps you in touch with the pulse of the community, its needs and desires, which often can be projected to other locales. Having local ties also enables you to keep up with trends, developments, and important local concerns.

In their rush to go national, most people overlook the local scene. Although the Internet has made it easier, it's usually difficult to expand your business when you haven't developed a strong local base. However, some people become too comfortable locally and never reach beyond their base, and this limits their growth. Try to bridge both areas.

Special background and interest groups, such as religious, ethnic, gender-based groups and those based on hobbies or particular activities, can be great referral sources. People like to help those with whom they feel a connection. I love networking with women. I feel that we have similar insights and feelings; networking with women-oriented groups is high on my list.

If you market authentic Mexican food, join the Hispanic Chamber of Commerce. If you are a CEO, go to the Vistage Chief Executive Program (formerly the TEC Group) chapter in your town.

■ ■ ■ Industry Groups

Virtually all industries have associations that are ideal for networking. These groups sponsor meetings, conferences, trade shows, and conventions. Examples of industry associations are the American Medical Association, the American Bar Association, the Security Industry Association, and the Upper Valley Chinese Engineers Association, among many others.

Network with members of your industry; get to know your peers. Sharing information, experiences, and insights with your colleagues will boost your visibility and increase your knowledge. Peers refer work to business colleagues when they have more work than they can handle, have customer or client conflicts, or need special or additional talents or help.

Referrals have more strength when practitioners in your discipline make them. They know the best people, the people who are reliable, and the people who can be trusted on specific projects; they don't make referrals lightly. When you want the best surgeon, your family doctor, another surgeon, or a member of the hospital staff is usually a good place to start.

Become a star in your industry. It will give you the best kind of visibility in the most relevant circles and boost your brand. Being a star will position you as an expert, and that usually enables you to receive more and higher-paying work.

Go against the grain; industry groups are ideal for cross-marketing. The few men I've seen at eWomenNetwork meetings not only stand out, they do extremely well. Cross-market if you can do so comfortably, but don't force your way into a group where you don't fit and are not wanted.

■ ■ ■ Structured Groups

Numerous groups exist either primarily or largely for networking and to promote business referrals. Most of these groups are privately owned, profit-making businesses that require you to pay substantial fees to attend their events. I call these organizations structured networking groups.

My experience has been that structured networking groups can be highly productive and beneficial. I've made many excellent contacts at structured groups, some of whom have become close friends and longtime strategic business associates.

Some of the most successful structured networking groups are eWomenNetwork (www.ewomennetwork.com), CEO Space LLC (www.ibiglobal.com), Business Networking International (BNI; www.bni.com), and LeTip International (www.letip.com). All these groups are designed to promote referrals.

Most structured groups hold sessions that are focused solely on networking and passing along referrals. Since these organizations frequently change their names, locations and merge, check their Web sites for the latest information about them.

■ ■ ■ Referral and Resource Groups

Form your own group. I had great success with referral and resource groups (RRGs), which are also called mastermind groups. In RRGs the members are dedicated to looking for and passing on opportunities that could help the other members. In RRGs the organizers choose the group's members and set the group's rules.

My most successful and enjoyable RRG was the Circle of Eight. It consisted of eight professional speakers. We had different specialties but provided complementary products and services and marketed to similar customers. Circle members were based throughout the country and in Canada, and that provided expanded opportunities for each of us.

When a circle member came across a lead, he or she immediately e-mailed it to the other members so that they could get a jump on those of interest. When members received leads, they could categorize, file, and track them quickly. Each month members were required to give at least two leads, two referrals, and one resource. Under our definitions, a lead was a tip that could create financial remuneration, a resource was someone or something that might provide help, and a strategic referral could help a member without involving payment.

Every month the circle held highly structured 30-minute meetings by phone that were run by the member we designated the facilitator. We all took turns being the facilitator. During our phone sessions, members brainstormed, asked and answered questions, and exchanged ideas. Each member summarized the state of his or her business, its recent developments, and its prospects. Then each recounted how many leads, resources, or strategic referrals he or she had given the other members. Discussions were held about members' needs, projects of possible interest, and ways each member could help.

The Circle of Eight was successful because the members liked, respected, and trusted one another. They also were happy to be associated with one another. They all worked hard to help the other members succeed.

RRGs tend to be short-lived because over time the members move in different directions. They all have different needs and are subject to demands that change. People get busy, focus on other interests, and become less committed.

Although the RRGs I joined lasted only two or three years, they were highly productive. They enabled me to form strong relationships that have gotten me lots of business. Don't avoid RRGs because they won't last. Everything has a life span and purpose. Give it a try, enjoy it as long as it is productive for you, and then move on. With RRGs, you must be clear about what you want. When an RPG no longer is helping you, be clear about that and move on.

▪ ▪ ▪ Starting Your Own Group

Create a networking group to advance your agenda. Decide on the size and structure and who you would like to invite. Design your group to be whatever you want: Host a group at your home that will share a couple of pizzas or rent a hall, invite a speaker, and conduct structured training sessions.

When I cowrote *Networking Magic*, we came across numerous groups that people had started to support their businesses or their favorite causes or just for fun, support, entertainment, information, or social interaction. They were of all sizes and existed for all purposes. In fact, they often served multiple purposes.

Regardless of how you do it, get together with other people. Meet them on a regular basis or just once in a while, but connect with them. Talk with them, interact with them, and get to know them. Learn who they are and what they do. Tell them about yourself, your business, and the benefits you can offer them and how they will enhance their lives.

Action Plan

1. What three items should you consider before joining an organization to network?

   _____

   _____

   _____

2. Where are good places to meet people at networking events, and how can you start conversations there?

   _____

   _____

   _____

   _____

   _____

3. What industry associations should you consider joining?

   _____

   _____

   _____

   _____

   _____

4. How could you create a group similar to my Circle of Eight, and who would be in it?

   _____

   _____

   _____

   _____

   _____

7

First Impressions

This chapter will cover:

- Fuller presentations
- Keeping it fresh
- Preparation
- Event protocol
- Meeting protocol
- Sending questions

IMMEDIATELY MAKE A GREAT first impression by introducing yourself with a sound bite. Use the sound bite to create a solid connection with important new contacts quickly.

Your sound bite is your verbal business card. It's the introduction that tells others several things:

- Who you are
- What you do
- The specific benefits you can provide

Here are some examples:

"I'm Dr. Delicato, DDS. In my chair you have no pain, no drugs, no anxiety—just healthy teeth and a radiant smile."
"My portraits let you preserve those beautiful moments of you and your family and treasure them for life."
"I bring delicious, hot, healthy meals to your door at your convenience and at your price."

A sound bite is a vital tool that clearly announces that you're a prepared, focused, and articulate professional who can help people.

When you create your sound bite, make it come from the heart. Try following these steps:

1. List what you do. Write the first thoughts that come to your mind. Don't worry about their length or complexity. Be descriptive and concentrate on getting information down.
2. Focus on the value you provide to customers or clients rather than the process you use. Explain what you deliver. For example, if you sell 1,000-count Egyptian sheets on eBay, don't tell people, "I sell sheets on eBay." Instead, say, "I help people sleep like royalty in the most luxurious sheets." Ask your top customers for feedback on your pitch.
3. When you complete your list, circle each descriptive word.
4. Transfer all the circled words to a separate sheet of paper and place them in the order of their importance to the customers or clients you want to reach.
5. Review each word to see if it is the most descriptive and colorful. If it is not, substitute a more graphic, illustrative, or hard-hitting word.
6. Work all the words on your list into a lively sentence or two. Make sure that it's clear, describes what you do, and is attention-grabbing. Stress the problems you can solve and the benefits you can provide. If possible, make it witty and clever, but not at the expense of clarity.

Practice your sound bite aloud. Try to recite it in less than 30 seconds. Then, when you can do that, knock off another 10 to 15 seconds. Experiment with differing rhythms and intonations to develop a flowing rhythm. Recite your sound bite to others and get their input on the content of your message and your delivery.

Present your sound bite with passion and enthusiasm. When you believe your sound bite, others will too. Vary your sound bite. Make minor changes so that it will sound natural and convincing and be appropriate in different situations.

■ ■ ■ Fuller Presentations

After you've given your sound bite, contacts often want to know more about you, your goods and/or services, and their benefits. Be ready to answer their questions and make a fuller presentation. Contacts may want more information then and there or want to communicate with you by phone, by e-mail, or in face-to-face meetings.

■ ■ QUESTIONS

Before you meet with anyone, anticipate that person's concerns and the questions that person might ask that are specific to his or her field. If you hold yourself out as an expert, you must be able to answer every question fully. Learn that by following these steps:

1. *Identifying the four, five, or six questions you continually hear.* People tend to have the same general concerns, and so they usually ask the same basic questions. Note what those questions are and also keep track of those which differ.
2. *Exploring how to answer each commonly asked question best.* Write a simple conversational one- to three-sentence answer to each question. Word your answers in alternative ways and for different prospects or groups. When you

write your answers, make sure to make them as appealing as spoken words, not like you're reading a speech or a brochure. Write conversational copy that is simple and direct.

3. *Obtaining the answers to less commonly asked questions.* Finding the answers will improve your expertise and understanding, and you may be able to work some of the information into your answers to the commonly asked questions or your full presentation.

4. *Finding practice partners.* Get together with friends or businesspeople who are in similar positions. Then find time to practice answering questions and making fuller presentations to them.

■ ■ FULLER PRESENTATIONS

Expand on your sound bite but still keep your presentation brief: two to three sentences that take 15 to 30 seconds to recite. Cover all the main points you should make without wasting your contacts' time. Expect contacts to question you and be ready to respond promptly.

Structure your presentation in three parts: (1) the opening, (2) the core, and (3) the close.

Opening

The opening is your introduction. It should state your qualifications and experience briefly and create interest in the core. "I began designing hardware for IBM and rose to chief designer before I started this firm." Since your opening is just an introduction, not the central focus of your presentation, be brief.

Core

This is the most important part of your presentation because it states what you do and how it will help your contact. Explain the benefits your goods or services will provide to the person with whom you are speaking as specifically as possible. Prepare this portion of your presentation by doing the following:

- Making a list of the key points you want to make.
- Being direct, specifically covering each point, and staying focused.
- Not hemming and hawing, dancing around, or trying to be cute or clever. Focus on quickly and clearly giving information.
- Clearly explaining:
  - What you do.
  - How it can benefit them, their friends, and their associates. When possible, quantify the benefits in terms of time, effort, money, increased productivity, and market share. When you state how much money can be made or saved, people will listen.
  - What you need from your contacts and how they can help.

Close

Briefly recap the benefits you can provide, make arrangements to follow up with your contact, and thank him or her. Schedule a time to speak or meet again and clarify what will be discussed. Double-check all times, dates, and contact information.

Confirm all arrangements you made via e-mail as soon as you can. If either of you agreed to obtain further information or take specific action, confirm in your e-mail that those items will be attended to.

Personalize your presentation. Try to relate it to your contact so that it will sound more personal, focused, and relevant but less canned. Nothing is worse than listening to a pitch you know has been made a million times before. Drop in a few current or personalized references; make sure that they are appropriate and don't take away or detract from your presentation. Don't go overboard.

During your presentation, expect your contact to have comments and questions. Answer all questions immediately. Then promptly return to the main points you want to make. Having a written list of the main points helps me refocus after interruptions.

Make sure that all the information you present is relevant. Some people trade on old stories that may be interesting or funny but are not relevant. Be more businesslike; focus on the here and now. If you have a great backstory, save it for a time when it will have more relevance and impact.

A woman at a conference introduced herself to me and began telling me about her personal history, emphasizing her troubles. Finally, she got to the point and asked me for advice on a business problem. When she finished, I asked, "Why are you telling me stories that happened fifteen years ago? They have nothing to do with your current business."

"That's exactly my problem," she admitted. "I have too much baggage, and it keeps me from getting to the heart of my present story."

Your background—your personal history—may be fascinating, and it certainly contributed to who you are. However, if your story keeps you from communicating effectively, ditch it. Giving background can be helpful—it can set the table, provide context, and prepare listeners for the points you want to stress—but it should not obscure the essential information that you should relate.

Break the ice, warm up listeners with a short sentence or two, but then get to the information you wish to emphasize. Get to the heart of the matter quickly or you can bore your listeners to death.

Timing and flexibility are crucial. At times, a full presentation can be inappropriate. For instance, if you're with a group of people who are laughing and telling stories, launching into your presentation may not be wise. If you're at a mixer where you have a 10-second intro, don't make a prolonged pitch. Rely on your instincts and intuition to adjust your presentation as needed.

■ ■ ■ Keeping It Fresh

Don't fall into the rut of constantly introducing yourself and delivering your message in the same way. Change it as often as you can to keep it fresh and current. You don't have to change everything; just substitute some words, phrases, or ideas.

Be topical. Work in something about the weather, the traffic, or the event you're attending. Link it to recent news, developments, and trends—anything that will break the mold and make it more current and personal.

"It doesn't take a lot to make people feel that you're talking directly to them," the comic juggler Owen Morse discloses, "but it's important that you do. If you put on the same show or say the same things without making reference to where you are, your surroundings, and whom you're addressing, it's going to fall flat. If you mention the company, people, or area's name; some current issues or news; inside jokes or information; or relevant observations, it will make your audience feel that you are speaking directly to them."

"Frequently, we perform before groups that don't get the credit they deserve, such as nurses." Morse continues. "Or we may perform for audiences where rivalries exist, so we try to work that in. We have a routine where Jon [Morse's partner] explains to the audience how he will juggle six rings. He gives it a big buildup and stresses how difficult it will be for him. As he speaks, he tosses the rings to me, and I actually do all the juggling while Jon takes all the credit. At the end of the routine, Jon asks me a question, and I say, 'All I know is that I'm playing the part of the nurse and you're playing the part of the surgeon,' which brings down the house and bonds us with the audience. We have spun this routine for sales and marketing, management and labor, and other rivalries," Morse reveals.

When you customize your presentations, it makes it clear that you created something specially for the people you are addressing, which is flattering to them. Even if the changes are minuscule, the fact that you attempted to add some personal material makes it special and helps you connect.

Customizing also has personal benefits. It forces you to stretch, search, and challenge yourself. It keeps you on your toes. When you continuously look for new connections, it broadens your knowledge and interests and helps your mind stay sharp. The more you learn, the more different types of connections you can make.

Preparation

Before you meet new people, know what you plan to say. Write it out and practice it on friends and family. Stand in front of a mirror and watch yourself. Record and listen to yourself reciting your sound bite and presentation.

Anticipate questions that could be asked. Practice stating your answers aloud. Listen to your voice. Feel whether it's strong, steady, and convincing. If it's not, keep practicing until it is.

Preparation is the best antidote to nervousness. Know your materials fully. Have people quiz you and ask them to be tough. When you really know your stuff, you still may have a few butterflies, but as soon as you begin speaking, your worries usually will disappear. If you know your material, believe in it, and concentrate on convincingly expressing it; that generally will allay your fears.

Make a list of your most important points. I find it preferable to list the most important points rather than trying to memorize them.

Then, when I speak, I'm more natural and extemporaneous. If someone asks a question or interrupts, I don't get thrown. I simply address it and then return to my list and continue.

Working from a list rather than a memorized script helps me be more spontaneous. I can make asides and work in topical comments that relate to the person or group I'm with, recent news, developments in the industry or locally, or even the weather.

Always have a supply of business cards with you. When you attend events, place the cards in a purse or pocket that you can access easily so that you can hand them out quickly. Be prepared to distribute them liberally. Also carry a small blank pad or notebook to write down important information and, of course, carry a pen.

Before meetings or events, I make it a point to read several newspapers, including at least one from the local area. They give me information that often comes in handy and enables me to participate in more conversations.

■ ■ ■ CONNECTING LINK ■ ■ ■

Arrive early and check out the scene. I like to arrive at events 15 to 20 minutes early. Frequently, they are still setting up and I can identify the movers and shakers and those who are putting on the event. I never get in their way but always smile, say hello, and tell them not to worry about me because I can wait. They can introduce you to important people when those people arrive, before others try to monopolize them.

When you arrive early, it's easier to network with those who are already present. It's more comfortable to start a conversation before the hordes arrive, and those conversations can be more productive and have fewer interruptions.

I try to walk around and learn the layout; that can save me time when the event is in full swing. I discover where sessions will be held and where the restrooms, food, and good areas for cell phone reception are.

When appropriate, I start conversations with staff members, asking them about the event, the guests, the presentations, and who I should try to meet. If they have strong suggestions, I ask if they can introduce me. Staff personnel are often important members of the organization who will help you during the event and afterward.

Some organizations will send you a list of the attendees before the events. When they do, I always see who I know. Then I think if I have any questions for them or any articles, information, or other items that might interest them. When I see the name of someone on a list whom I don't know but would like to meet, I try to think who could introduce us or plan how I could introduce myself.

▪ ▪ ▪ Event Protocol

When you meet or are introduced to others at events, take your time. Start with some pleasantries and don't immediately launch into your sound bite or pitch. I usually say, "Hello, nice to meet you," and listen. I don't speak about myself until I'm asked, which generally occurs in short order.

When I'm asked about myself, it gives me license to recite my sound bite and speak. I try to be direct and brief. As I say my piece, I try to observe their reactions. Then I ask if they have questions and answer those they raise. I try to be loose and informal, and that helps everyone relax.

At events, I try to limit the length of my conversations and not get bogged down. My objective is to meet a lot of new people, and so I try to speak with different people and groups. If I feel that I have been in a conversation too long, I break away by smiling and politely saying, "Excuse me. It was nice meeting you. I hope to see you later." Then I leave.

Before you leave a conversation, give people your business card and ask for theirs. If the subject of being in contact again is raised, write the relevant information on their business cards or in a notebook. If you contact them after the event, do so within the next few days, before the conversation slips their minds.

■ ■ ■ Meeting Protocol

Meetings that contacts have arranged or played a role in can be face to face or by phone. Before these meetings, I make a list of all the points I want to cover. Then I follow these steps:

- I make sure to call or arrive on time.
- I'm direct and specific. I quickly thank them for their time, tell them about me, and explain how they can help. If they're forthcoming and offer help, I write down names, numbers, addresses, instructions, or other information.
- When those I meet with are not helpful, I still express my thanks and make sure never to sound sarcastic, ungrateful, or annoyed. I never argue, cajole, or try to change their minds. I try to be polite and understanding and salvage something from the contact, even if it's just leaving a good impression. If you hit a wall, ask if your contact can suggest someone else you could call.
- If people want to chat, give them some room but don't let them go on forever or divert you from your point. Stay focused and gently bring them back to your main point. Always be brief and polite. Impress people with your professionalism, your ability to get to the point quickly, and remain on track.

At meetings, begin your conversation by thanking contacts for their time and stress that you will be brief. Then speak your piece. When you're direct and concise, people usually relax and are more forthcoming because they appreciate your respect for their time. Although they may not satisfy your requests, they may remember your professionalism and consideration, and that could pay dividends at a subsequent time.

■ ■ ■ Sending Questions

Opinions are mixed about sending your questions beforehand to the contacts you will be meeting. Those in favor believe that it makes conversations more efficient, focused, and productive. Those opposed contend that questions ask busy people to do one more thing—read an e-mail—which adds to their jam-packed schedules.

If people want your questions in advance, definitely send them. Confirm how they want them sent and get their contact information. Then keep all correspondence brief. Here is an example:

> Dear Mr. Meyers:
>
> I'm really looking forward to speaking with you on Thursday. When we speak, I would like to address:
>
> 1. Whether you think I should join the Marketing Directors' Club.
> 2. What services I could provide to the people you refer.
> 3. The prices I should charge and your referral fees, if any.
>
> Thanks for your time!
>
> Jill

When your conversation has been completed, express your thanks and quickly leave or get off the phone. Follow up by sending a note of thanks. Again, I prefer to send handwritten notes because I think that makes a strong impression, especially since e-mail is so prevalent.

If someone gives you a lot of his or her time, a small gift could be apropriate: flowers, a box of candy, or something small. It doesn't have to be anything expensive—just a token to express your appreciation. Try to send what you think that person would like and would be good for him or her.

Action Plan

1. Write a sound bite for yourself.

_____

_____

_____

2. Write two alternative versions of your sound bite.

_____

_____

_____

3. Write a fuller presentation that you could recite in less than 30 seconds.

_____

_____

_____

_____

_____

_____

4. Customize your fuller presentation for contacts in the three specialty areas you are most likely to pitch.

_____

_____

_____

_____

_____

_____

_____

8

Goals, Intentions, and Strategies

This chapter will cover:

- Meeting new people
- Deepening relationships
- Accomplishing specific tasks
- Creating strategy
- Education-based marketing

IDENTIFY YOUR OBJECTIVES; know precisely what you want to achieve. When you're clear about your goals, you can explain them to others. If others understand what you need, they will be better able to help. The clearer you are about your goals, the more likely you are to create a plan that will accomplish them.

Before I attend meetings or events, I set goals. I decide what I would like to accomplish. Since meetings usually have specific agendas, I identify what I would like to achieve. Defining my goals helps me when I meet people later; it helps me focus by subconsciously keeping me on track.

For events, my goals usually break down into three broad categories. In most cases I want to do one of the following:

1. Meet new people
2. Deepen existing relationships
3. Accomplish specific tasks

Then I set more specific goals, which I call my intentions. For example, if I go to a two-hour event, one of my intentions will be to meet three new people. If I plan to go to an event where I know a lot of people, my intention may be to deepen my relationships with three people. Frequently, I have a number of intentions, including meeting new people, deepening relationships, accomplishing specific tasks, and generating a certain amount of business. In a meeting that lasts an hour and a half, connecting with three people is a realistic goal.

When you set goals to get referrals and build relationships, it's easy to be diverted. Other opportunities frequently come up that look more promising. I find that I'm most successful when I create a plan, develop a strategy, and stick with it. Here's an example:

- *Step 1: Define my targets.* Identify the people who are the most likely to buy my services.
- *Step 2: Select an approach.* Send a postcard to 50 potential customers informing them about my availability and the wonders my services can provide. I try to link my services to particular events of interest to them.
- *Step 3: Set targets.* Try to connect with a specific number of people. If I attend an event, I make it my goal to meet and schedule meetings with five new prospects to discuss my services.
- *Step 4: Follow through.* When they show interest, I promptly follow up because as time passes, they may not remember me. If I make and confirm appointments when I am still fresh in their minds, they are usually more responsive.

■ ■ ■ Meeting New People

Every business needs an influx of new clients and customers, and so I always try to meet people who could be potential clients, resources, or referral sources. I try to find them through new organizations and those in which I'm already involved.

Usually, people tell me about organizations or I read or hear about them. If a certain group arouses my interest, I try to contact people who I think would know about them. In most cases, someone in my network can fill me in. My primary interest is to learn about the types of people who are in the group: who they are, what they do, and why they attend. Then I learn when and where the group meets, what its meetings or events are like, and how long they take.

I love going to new organizations because for me it's virgin soil and there are many new people to meet. Frequently, I run into someone I know who can introduce me and tell people about me.

My favorite places to meet new people are the traditional spots; for me they are extremely effective:

- *On lines.* It's natural and comfortable to strike up conversations while I'm waiting in line. A brief comment or complaint about the line, a compliment about what the person is wearing, or a statement about the event can open the door. Since people are just standing and waiting, they usually welcome the opportunity to talk and make new contacts. I've made contacts on lines who became my friends. They worked with me, sent me business, and invited me to stay at their homes.
- *In the ladies' room.* Most women are friendly and chatty, and restrooms are natural places to connect. Women often make small talk while they check their hair and makeup. I find that most women instinctively look at other women to see who is next to them and how they look, and so it's natural and comfortable for them to talk.
- *Where food is served.* People sneak away and escape to areas where food is served because it gives them a break

from the action and helps them relax. When you wander into these areas, it's natural to start conversations with brief comments such as "Workshops always make me hungry" and "Those muffins look homemade."

Debbie Allen built her network by concentrating on meeting experts. Her favorite way to meet them is by arriving early at events where they are speaking and approaching them before they speak. "No one bothers speakers before they go on," Allen observes, "so you have them all to yourself. After they speak, everyone wants to talk to them, but before they go on stage, you can meet them, get to know them, get personal attention, and have your picture taken with them."

■ ■ ■ ■ Deepening Relationships

Since referrals are a large part of my business, I make a special effort to nourish or deepen my referral relationships. I select events that I know certain people will attend. However, I usually don't spend a great deal of time looking for them or waiting while they are speaking with others.

I've found that being flexible is more efficient. When possible, I review the attendees' list before the event, or I do it as soon as I arrive, which is another reason to arrive early at events. Then I note which people I would like to contact; I make a wish list.

At the event, I play it by ear. If I see people on my list, I approach them. If I don't, I speak with those I come across. Usually it's just a matter of timing and who you see.

Networking events can be like speed dating. People rush past each other, give quick greetings, and see how many folks they can acknowledge. Usually they just say, "Hello, how are you? I'm doing great. See you later."

To deepen relationships, I stop and talk with people. I try to catch up on how they have been, ask about their latest projects, and find out what is on the drawing board. Then I fill them in on me. Usually, three to five minutes is more than enough time to make a solid connection, exchange business cards, and agree to speak again about whatever should be followed up.

At events, it's often more productive to concentrate on making contacts and then setting up appointments to speak with those people later, when you both have more time. If, however, someone shows great interest when you meet, take it as far as you can. Don't lose the opportunity.

When you speak with people at events, concentrate on how you can help them instead of simply selling yourself. Ask what they need and think about how you or someone you know can help. I find that when I extend myself, most people reciprocate. Therefore, I make the first move and don't wait for them to volunteer their help.

When I come across someone I want to speak with at greater length, I arrange a time when we can meet and talk without interruption. We may agree to meet later or have dinner or drinks.

At most events, when the main meetings have ended, people get together for drinks. These after-event soirees are ideal for spending time and deepening relationships.

▪ ▪ ▪ CONNECTING LINK ▪ ▪ ▪

For years, I've attended National Speakers Association (NSA) events and been a featured speaker. These events usually feature the same cast of characters, many of whom I have done business with and come to know well. Thus, at NSA affairs, one of my intentions is to deepen my relationships.

Before the last four-day NSA winter meeting, I printed the attendees list and circled the names of people (1) whom I hadn't seen for a while and with whom I wanted to connect, (2) with whom I wanted to deepen my relationship, (3) whom I just wanted to say hello to, and (4) whom I wanted to interview for this book. I must have circled 50 to 60 names.

The first evening, during the opening sessions, I stayed in my room phoning the rooms of everyone on my list. All I said was, "Hello, this is Jill Lublin. I can't wait to see you. I hope that you are doing well and I'll see you in the next few days."

Over the next few days, countless people thanked me for my call. Most of them were touched that I took the time and made the effort to contact them. I had conversations with some of them and made plans with others. Even though I didn't speak with everyone on my list, my phone calls made a great impression on them.

Small touches make a difference; they provide a positive impression that people remember. People cannot send you referrals if they don't remember you, so find ways to be memorable.

When you find people to form strategic alliances with, "serve them in an extraordinary way before you ask anything of them," Tommy Newberry teaches. "Find out what they need, what would be of value to them, and offer to help them get it. Don't charge them; just help them. Do them a favor. Put out far more than you expect to receive and do it well in advance of the time the relation is formalized or becomes or established."

"Then, when you want to formalize the relationship," Newberry notes, "you won't have to sell because you've laid the groundwork. And he will be willing to help you because of how you've served him."

Newberry believes in extending yourself to people as a way of operating and as a way of living your life. "Constantly help others. Plant seeds and build alliances," he recommends. "Ninety-nine percent of people will help you if you help them first. The idea is to establish a helpful, serving attitude. When you help others, you have laid the groundwork because you gave something of value."

◼ ◼ ◼ Accomplishing Specific Tasks

When I know that someone will be attending an event, I may arrange to meet with him or her to accomplish a specific objective. Frequently, these are work sessions. For example, if we are working on a project together, we may want to bring each other up to date and decide what additional steps we should take. I may have completed a report that I would like the other person to review, or we might explore the possibilities of jointly handling a future venture.

When I have specific tasks to complete, I make it a point to set aside an exact time for the task. If I don't, something is bound to come up and the opportunity can be lost. Or we may find that we don't have enough time to deal with the matter fully and properly.

Always confirm meetings to accomplish tasks. If you arranged to meet someone at a certain time, send a confirming e-mail. If the event will run for a day or less, send a confirming e-mail a day or two before the event. If the event will run more than one day, send an e-mail a day or two before the event and reconfirm with an e-mail or call during the event.

◼ ◼ ◼ Creating Strategy

When you attend a networking meeting or event, devise a clear strategy. Know exactly what you want to accomplish and create a plan to see it through.

In devising your strategy, do the following things:

- Reaffirm your objectives. Identify what you want to achieve in both the short term and the long term.
- Set financial targets. Decide how much business you hope to generate from each meeting or event. If you don't make financial projections, you can't judge whether attending the meeting or event was successful.

- Select your targets. Decide how many people you want to meet and what connections you wish to make. Then identify who they are. What do you have in common with them?
- Plan how you will approach them. Practice exactly what you plan to say until you can rattle it off in 10 to 15 seconds. Be direct, clear, and brief.
- Have brochures, handouts, business cards, and other supporting materials to distribute. People are busy. Show concern for their time by giving them your card and materials and asking if you can call them to follow up.
- Be able to expand on your 10- to 15-second opening if asked and be prepared to answer all questions.
- Prepare specific questions that you can ask to start conversations: Why are you here? Is this the first time you have attended? Do you need or know of people who need a strategic business consultant? What other good networking events have you enjoyed? To get specific referrals, be specific.

During events, look at name tags. Find out what kind of business a person is in. Would this person be a good connection for you, your customers, your clients, or people in your network? Besides looking for yourself, think about who could help your customers, clients, and network members. Networking is a reciprocal arrangement: If you help others, they usually will help you. Frequently, you have to start the ball rolling by referring business to them. When you do that often enough, it pays dividends.

You never know what connections exist and how far people's networks extend. If you see someone at an event who is a painting contractor, don't automatically disqualify her. If you can't connect directly through her business, you may fit with a member of her network. At an event, I actually met a painting contractor who was involved with an organization that was looking for speakers. We spoke and hit it off, and I was invited to speak to his group. Don't make too many assumptions.

■ ■ ■ Education-Based Marketing

Chet Holmes, author of the best-selling *The Ultimate Sales Machine* (Portfolio, 2007) and chairman and CEO of Chet Holmes International, champions one of my favorite strategies: education-based marketing. It's predicated on giving customers the most and best information about their goods or services.

Education-based marketing works because people are barraged constantly with sales pitches, arm-twisting, and BS. They've heard every promise and every claim and want to decide for themselves. They want enough information to make their own decisions, so give them what they want.

Research your markets; learn about your prospects' industries and why those businesses succeed and fail. "Start all presentations with terrific information about the prospect's market or area of interest that will be of value to it," Holmes suggests. "It immediately positions you as an expert who knows more than they do. When a prospect sees that you have more expertise, the control and influence switches. You gain the prospect's respect and create a much deeper level of rapport," he notes. "Then when you begin to sell, your credibility is at such a high level that you'll land many more sales."

Don't contact a prospect and say, "Hi, I'm from *XYZ Gazette* and would like to talk to you about advertising in our newspaper," Holmes warns. Eighty percent of the prospects will not be interested.

Instead state, "Hi, I'm with *XYZ Gazette*. We've conducted research and have developed a success program for restaurants. Are you familiar with it?" When they answer no, reply, "We found five reasons why restaurants fail and seven reasons why they succeed. Would you be interested in seeing that information?" According to Holmes, this approach reverses the acceptance rate to 8 of 10 from 2 of 10, a 400 percent increase.

One of the major reasons businesspeople fail is that they are poor marketers, Holmes has found. Thus, whoever can give the most information will dominate the market.

"If you sell shoes, know everything about shoe construction, about feet, about fashion, and how shoes interact with fashion," Holmes stresses. "The people who work in most shoe stores don't know any of those things. They only know that you need size nine and they run to the back to get it. However, if when they return they inform the customer 'that there are 214,000 nerve endings in your feet that connect to every organ of your body,' they seize control of the sale."

At phone stores, the salespeople can't answer your questions, Holmes laments. "If I owned a phone store, my people would be extremely well educated. They could answer every question, tell people about shortcuts and how to use the phone. We would offer free courses to customers on how to maximize the use of your cell phone. I'd put it right in my ads: 'Take Our Free Course on 48 Ways to Use Your Cell Phone' and 'Don't Miss Cell Phone Use Made Easy,' " he adds.

"One of the biggest mistake businesses make is only thinking how to close the sale. Instead, they should concentrate on winning the customer," Holmes observes.

To illustrate this point, Holmes told me about two furniture stores that opened in the same town at the same time. In four years, Store A grew 40 percent and Store B grew 600 percent. Store A concentrated on selling furniture, and Store B focused on sales but also promoted itself to its clientele. Its salespeople asked customers if they had been to the store before; told them about its history, business approach, and values; and explained its programs and benefits.

For example, Store B's salespeople told their customers, "Our store was founded in 1947 by two brothers to provide the best value. We select only the sturdiest, longest-lasting environmentally friendly products. Our staff knows more about furniture and its construction than anyone else. And we have free programs to teach you about design, care, repair, replacement, moving, use, plus much more. Finally, we have free delivery and will send someone to your home to repair scratches and other damage at no charge."

Holmes points out that many stores provide similar services but rarely mention them to their customers. The problem is that sales reps are not trained to provide this information. In Store B, however, they all attend weekly sales and strategy training on how they should always work a strategic objective into their conversations with customers.

Find great information to give prospects by looking at industry developments over time, Holmes suggests. You can find trends and facts that others may not have spotted. Your research can reveal the changes that have occurred in markets, customers, methods, materials, distribution, pricing, competition, and many other areas. Then tell prospects key facts that relate to them.

If you need specific business information, Holmes recommends Empire Research Group (www.empireresearchgroup.com), which conducts research on all industries.

Action Plan

1. List the specific goals you would want to achieve if you attended a large networking event.

   _____

   _____

   _____

2. List the people with whom you would like to deepen your relationships.

   _____

   _____

   _____

3. Describe the strategy that you would use at a networking event.

   _____

   _____

   _____

   _____

   _____

4. Explain how you can use education-based marketing in your business.

   _____

   _____

   _____

   _____

   _____

   _____

9

Cultivate the Media

This chapter covers:

- The media's rules
- Press releases
- Being prepared
- Becoming a media resource
- Media lists
- Categorizing
- Following up

GET NOTICED BY the media. If you attract the media's attention, it will tell the world about you, your exploits, and your achievements and sing the praises of your goods and services. Become a media star because nothing can build your business as quickly and as well as media coverage.

People believe what they see, hear, and read in the media. Unlike advertising, which everyone knows is hype, information reported by the media is taken as fact; it's considered news and accepted as being reliable. Media coverage can put your business on the map. A favorable story about you or a radio or television feature can bring you customers galore.

The key to getting media coverage is to be prepared, be proactive, and understand the rules. You also must be patient and persistent. Let me explain.

- *Being prepared.* Know what is interesting about your story—what currently interests people—and connect with the public. The media are in the news business, and if your story is newsworthy, it will interest the media. The media love to cover stories about money, sex, and health because they think that is what their audience wants. The media are attracted to people who overcame obstacles and great odds, took a unique approach, fought long and valiantly, and wouldn't quit.
- *Being proactive.* You can't wait for the media to find you; you have to be assertive and contact them. You also must be creative by making your story or items in it relevant to the public's current interests. Always be aware of the latest trends and developments and the way your story relates to them. Then shape your story accordingly.
- *Understanding the rules.* The media operate according to their own rules. Those rules are based on the need to provide informative and entertaining news continuously.

Kate Adamson, a healthy 33-year-old mother of two, had a double brain stem stroke that totally incapacitated her. She could not move or speak, and doctors inserted breathing and feeding tubes and assumed that she was in a coma. However, Kate could hear, think, and feel pain, although she could not communicate or respond. After two weeks in that state, followed by months of hospitalization, she showed slow but steady progress. Kate miraculously recovered, which is the subject of her book, *Paralyzed but Not Powerless* (SevenLocks Press, 2007).

When the Terri Schiavo story broke, Kate and her husband, attorney Steven Klugman, recognized that Kate had the unique ability to provide knowledge and insights that no one else could. She could describe what it was like to be in what doctors considered a coma. Kate and Steven contacted the media. Steven would call and ask, " 'Are you covering this story, because we have an interesting angle?' At first, they didn't want to talk, so I quickly had to tell them the angle. Then they became intrigued." Kate then went on every major show in the country.

■ ■ ■ The Media's Rules

The media constantly need and always are searching for new stories and information for their audiences. If you can help supply it, the media will love you and tell your story. Although the media need you as much as you need them, you must play by the media's rules.

■ ■ ■ CONNECTING LINK ■ ■ ■

Although media relationships are mutually beneficial, they are not equal; the media have the upper hand. Everyone wants his or her story publicized, and the media control whether, when, and how those stories are told. Since the media can pick and choose, package your story in a way that the media think will interest their audience.

To be covered by the media, you must follow its rules:

1. You must attract their attention. Everyone is vying for the media's attention, and the media have a limited amount of space. Every day, each member of the media is inundated with press releases and pitches for potential stories. Show that your story is newsworthy and will be of interest to the audience.
2. You are nothing more than a resource for the media. When the media are interested in your story, you will be their

best and dearest friend. Members of the media will call you constantly and try to endear themselves to you. However, as soon as your story has been told, the media will disappear; they will be off and running to the next story and will stop contacting you. It's not personal; it's just the nature of the business, the way it works.

3. The media can change the rules, but you can't. From the moment you make contact with the media, everything is in their hands. The media may show interest initially but go no further. They can change your story or even kill it at the very last minute. Since the media's main mission is to convey the news, your story can be displaced by newly breaking developments; it can be dropped and not picked up. The media and their needs always have the last word.

"The reality is that the media is very cruel, very short on memory," Steven Klugman notes. "When you are having your fifteen minutes, they will send limousines and go out of their way to please you. But when your story is no longer hot, no one has the time of day for you. But you can't resent it," Klugman counsels. "You have to understand and try to plan your next move."

If you try to buck the system, you will get nowhere fast. Be patient, be understanding, and play by the media's rules. When the media don't produce as promised, don't be difficult or demanding. Hide your disappointment and anger and move on. Leave the media impressed that you are a professional who understands the rules because some of their members may appreciate your behavior and show their thanks at a later time. If, however, you make life difficult for them, they will remember that, and it could come back to haunt you.

Press Releases

Learn to write press releases to send to the media. Write lively one-page releases that will grab the media's attention and interest them in your story. We call these releases one sheets. It's essential that your releases be brief, attention-grabbing, and straight to the point because people in the media constantly receive press releases and don't have time to read them all thoroughly. If you send e-mail releases, don't exceed one computer screen.

Begin each press release with a dynamic, eye-catching headline. If your headline isn't strong, your media contacts probably will not read the release. In a short, concise one-line headline, state enough about your story to make the media want to read further to learn more about it. Tease them, whet their appetites, and draw them in.

Learn to write headlines by studying newspapers and magazines. See how their headlines are structured, worded, and phrased. Note the colorful graphic language and the tone they take. Then practice writing headlines that will interest the media in your story.

When you create headlines, remember that the media think that their audience is obsessed with three subjects: sex, money, and health. Whenever possible, link your story to those subjects.

After you write the headline, compose a lead sentence. That sentence can be similar to your sound bite and should not exceed two lines. Clearly state who you are, what you do, and the benefits you provide. Then add a sentence or two to explain further. The first paragraph of a press release should not exceed three or four sentences and should be able to stand alone.

Don't include too much detail in the first paragraph; just stress the major points. Then, in a subsequent paragraph or two, fill in the details. Include facts, statistics, quotes, endorsements, and brief anecdotes.

In the body of my press releases, I like to use bulleted one-line subheadings. Write your bullets like headlines. Bullets help readers move quickly to important information that you want to emphasize, so list all bulleted information in order of importance. See the two sample press releases below.

Be sure to include all your contact information in your press releases. If a release runs more than one page, include your contact information on each page.

For Immediate Release
National Association of Women Real Estate Investors
Contact: Lisa Miterko
(XXX) XXX-XXXX

Women Invest "Not To Lose" and Lose 73% of Income upon Loss of Spouse

(Denver, CO). Women lose 73 percent of their income when they lose their spouse through death, divorce, or desertion. Yet our culture continues to teach us to rely on our spouse to bring home the bacon. Wealth-building expert C. L. Osborn, founder of National Association of Women Real Estate Investors, creates simple solutions for women to become millionaires in 3 to 5 years. Osborn says, "I tell women: Ladies, a man is not a plan, no more than buying a lottery ticket is a retirement plan." The divorce rate is over 51 percent and women outlive men, so why do so many women leave the control of their financial destiny up to others? "Lack of education," says Osborn.

According to Osborn, there are three investor types in the world:

- People who do not invest at all, expecting someone else to take care of them
- People who invest not to lose, investing in CDs, mutual funds, stocks, etc.
- People who invest to win and take responsibility for their financial freedom

For women investors who want to win, Osborn says the best plan is learning to invest in real estate with people who do most of the work for you and help you with the money and credit issues. Then, she advises, develop a long-term strategy to make your money make you money.

A big believer in real estate, Osborn says, "You can get started with what I call monkey dust, which is little or no money or credit." Real estate offers women three substantial leveraging opportunities that other investment options do not:

- Invest in real estate without spending cash. In other words, investors can expect a return without putting money in. That's leverage.
- Refinance and use the proceeds used to reinvest in more real estate. That's called compounding.
- Grow your wealth with real estate appreciation while you live your life. That's called passive income, the key to becoming a multimillionaire.

C.L. Osborn

From an uneducated single mother to a multimillionaire real estate investor, C. L. Osborn simply conveys that the journey to financial freedom starts the minute you decide that you were destined for prosperity, not scarcity; for abundance, not lack; the freedom of being your own boss—without the limits of a job. Ms. Osborn is the author of the upcoming book *Wealth Formula One, Wise Women Invest in Real Estate and Tell Their Secrets,* based on her groundbreaking training formula. Ms. Osborn, CEO and founder of the National Association of Women Real Estate Investors, is also on the faculty of CEO Space, an international executive education organization.

FOR IMMEDIATE RELEASE

Contact: Jennifer

jenn@xxxxx.com

555-555-5555

Spending Money Will Make You Wealthy—Saving It Will Keep You Broke

(Victoria, British Columbia) The biggest stress in people's lives is money. In fact, a recent survey in the *New York Times* put the fear of running out of money in retirement ahead of the fear of terrorism. As a Certified Financial Planner with 16 years' experience, Tracy Piercy of MoneyMinding.com wants to give you easy things you can do today to reduce this stress and get your money working for you, rather than you working for your money.

If your entire financial plan in life is about cutting back, reducing expenses, increasing your savings, and increasing your investment returns in order to accumulate a large amount of money to draw on someday, you are setting yourself up for failure. Tracy teaches strategies beyond the conventional wisdom of simply cutting back and saving. Instead, she offers 3 solutions to help you find available money to spend:

- Start by using cash, not debit or credit you pay off each month—cash, cash, cash!
- Write down everything in your own handwriting about your financial goals and current money details: what you owe; what you own; and what your monthly expenses are. All the details need to be on one page to see exactly where you are and what needs to be done by when.

- The question is not that you cannot or will not find an answer. The question is how can you create the income you need to solve the problem? Do some brainstorming on paper about some creative ways to generate the income you need.

Tracy Piercy, CFP, is the president and founder of the MoneyMinding Makeover Membership, which offers step-by-step proven success principles, tools, ideas, and strategies integrated with practical financial planning tactics. With more than 16 years of experience in the financial industry, Tracy brings expertise in insurance, banking, and investing. Having been a top-producing investment advisor for one of Canada's largest investment firms, then experiencing great personal financial and personal loss, Tracy shares a collection of exercises on developing a mindset for financial success in her book *Englightened Wealth* and over 50 specific immediate action tips to help you expand the financial possibilities in your life in her new book, *The 12 Simple Steps of Money Minding.* She is an international speaker and has been featured on radio, TV, and print throughout North America.

For more information please contact:
Tracy Piercy
tracy@moneyminding.com

Being Prepared

Before you attempt to deal with the media, be prepared. Know your story inside out and know how to deliver it flawlessly. Be able to answer every imaginable question because the media will come up with some that are completely new. When your moment comes, convincingly sell your story and promote your goods and services because the opportunity may never come again.

Know your objective. When you deal with the media your two main objectives should be the following:

1. To tell your story clearly
2. To be invited back or receive more coverage

Know exactly what you're going to say. Write a script and list the three or four main points you want to make. Opening questions are frequently general and can give you openings to slide into your main points. Respond to the questions that are asked, and if the opportunity comes, work your main points in gracefully. Never force them. Anticipate questions that could be asked and, when appropriate, work in your major points.

If you're asked a question, never bluff. Admit that you don't know the answer but add that you will find it and get back to the host or interviewer with that information.

Take media training to maximize your opportunities. Most people never have dealt with the media, and so they try to learn as they go; that can be a big mistake. If you do poorly with an initial media contact, it could be your last. Learn exactly how to proceed.

Media training will teach you how to respond effectively to questions and leave the best impression. It will teach you how to be both entertaining and informative so that the media will love you and invite you back. Media training will show you how to please audiences, turn questions to your advantage, and deflect questions that could create problems.

Preparation is essential because when the media latch on to your story, they can get into a feeding frenzy. Everyone may want you at once. "We got about fifty calls a day," Kate Adamson disclosed. "So we become responders, not planners, and we didn't always make the best choices. We turned down great opportunities because we were exhausted."

Have a plan and be prepared to change it and adapt. In the thick of the blitz, amid all the demands, always focus on your mission: to tell your story. Before the media come calling, get help.

Have people on hand who can step in to help you capitalize on your opportunities.

Have a promotion plan in place and people who can help you carry it out because you can't do it all yourself. Script out everything for those four to five on-camera minutes so that you can be at your best.

■ ■ ■ Become a Media Resource

Endear yourself to the media by becoming a resource for them. Be accessible and go out of your way to provide them with solid, newsworthy information. "The press has been very kind to Craigslist because they know we are accessible and realize that we will give them straight information," Craig Newmark points out.

Take the initiative. Ask your media contacts what they are working on and refer them to any of your connections who could help them. Media outlets have calendars that list the projects they are developing. Ask your contacts what's on their calendars and volunteer to help even if you have no interest in or cannot benefit from the story.

When the media cover stories, they often include the opinions of experts. If you have a particular talent or expertise, offer your services as a media expert. Let them know that they can contact you at any time to get more in-depth information on the subject and then make sure that you are always available for them. If you also know others who would make outstanding media experts, tell your contacts about them.

Keep up with the media and be an information source. Inform your media contacts when you learn about items that might interest them. Track the careers of media members. Read their stories; watch and listen to their shows. Note their interests and the areas they cover and try to spot trends. Then, when you come across stories or people that could interest or help them, give them their names.

A few years ago I leased an electric car, which I loved. The lease agreement specified that after three years I was to receive another elec-

When you pitch stories or provide information to the media, everything must be correct. Verify all facts; double-check all dates, figures, and amounts. Fill in any gaps by conducting your own research and contact experts to get their slant. Make the media's job easier. Develop a reputation for being an excellent and reliable source who is helpful and good to work with.

Stay in contact with your media connections. Send them e-mails, updates, and announcements about you, your business, and new developments. Forward articles or interesting information to remind them of you.

tric car. However, the car company decided differently and informed me that when the term expired, it would cancel the lease. Instead of recycling my car and supplying me with another one as promised, it was going to crush my car and hundreds of other electric cars.

I was incensed. Here I was trying to make a difference by driving an electric car, but Detroit, which ironically is my hometown, didn't care. After getting nowhere and becoming more frustrated, I contacted the media. The San Francisco ABC-TV outlet jumped on the story. It sent a crew and filmed me driving my car, and it ran the story that evening.

Other media outlets, including *USA Today*, picked up the story. Suddenly I was not just Jill the author/speaker but Jill the electric-car advocate. Major environmental groups got involved and pressured the corporate giant not to destroy all the electric cars it had leased. And I'm happy to say that because of our efforts, over 200 electronic cars were saved.

Through this incident I made many great media contacts that have continued to be helpful. Strangers and people I hardly knew told me that they applauded my efforts. Although it was not my intention, I even got a few clients who came to me because they appreciated my concern about the environment.

▪ ▪ ▪ Media Lists

Organize your dealings with the media by creating a media list. A media list contains names, contact information, and other important facts about people in the media.

Include as many people as possible on your media list because any one of them could be interested in your story. Your list should contain the following information about each contact:

- Name
- Employer
- Street address
- E-mail address
- Office phone
- Cell phone
- Backup phone numbers
- Specialty areas
- How you got the name
- Common interests, backgrounds, experiences, and people
- Projects pitched, their outcomes, when they ran, and the results
- When you last were in contact
- Personal information such as families, interests, medical issues, and accomplishments
- Your comments, including summaries of your dealings with the contact

Update your complete media list at least once every three months. If you continually add to and update it, you quickly will build a comprehensive media list that will be a valuable asset.

People in the media move frequently, changing companies, positions, and even careers. When you hear about a change or development, update your list and send a brief note to your contact. For instance, do this when a contact is promoted, moves, or breaks a big story.

Excellent contact software is available that you could use for your media lists. These programs are easy to use and will keep you well organized.

■ ■ ■ Categorizing

Organize your media list alphabetically and divide it into categories. List your contacts by the type of media, such as print, radio, television, and the Internet; their specialty areas, including general news, business, entertainment, food, and sports; and geographical locations. You also can list them according to media outlets. Categorizing enables you to pinpoint your pitches more precisely and save time, money, and energy.

Also divide the entries on your media list according to their clout and helpfulness. I create three groups: my A, B, and C lists.

The A list should include the names of your top media contacts: those who can help you the most. They may be members of the national media, contacts who have helped and extended themselves for you, and contacts with major industry associations. Your A list will contain your most important media targets, the ones you will contact first.

Your B list will include the names of media contacts who are important but are not stars. They work for the second-level national media, outlets in large metropolitan areas, and people with major corporation and industry associations. Concentrate on developing your B list contacts and try to make them into A list contacts.

Your C list will include members of local, urban, and rural media. Although they don't have as much clout as those on your A and B lists, they can be extremely productive for you and usually will be easier to contact and more interested in your story. Again, work with your C list and try to promote those people to your B list.

■ ■ ■ Following Up

As I've stated, members of the media are busy and have constant demands on their time. Most are overworked and underpaid. When you try to contact them, you may get stuck with their voice mail or they may not respond to your e-mails. Therefore, you must follow up.

When a media contact doesn't get back to you, don't let the matter die. Lack of response doesn't necessarily mean that your contact is not interested in your story or that it isn't good. He or she may be deeply involved with another matter and not have the opportunity to contact you.

After a day or two, call or e-mail back, but don't be a pest. Leave gentle messages that indicate that you understand that person's plight and are willing to be patient. For example, say, "I know how jammed you are, but this story seems ideal for you."

When you follow up, clearly state your name, why you're contacting that person, and how you can be contacted. Make your pitch brief. Deliver your sound bite or state the most essential facts. Don't go into long-winded spiels; be brief. If a contact is interested, he or she will get back to you. Here are a few tips:

- If you have a difficult name, spell it slowly.
- Repeat phone numbers or e-mail addresses twice.
- Be polite and understanding and thank your contact for his or her time.

When people call or e-mail the media to follow up on items, they often say they are calling to check if the contact received their package. Don't leave it at that; also ask if the contact understood everything and if he or she has any questions or needs any further information.

When you finally connect with a contact, be precise about what you want. State that you would like an article written or want to appear on a show. Regardless of what you get, be polite and state your appreciation even if you do not receive all that you had hoped.

Getting commitments from the media can take a while. Expect to make at least 10 calls. If contacts don't respond, don't get exasperated. Keep calling; be pleasant, polite, and understanding. People in the media respect persistence, but the quality of potential stories comes first.

Create a follow-up log. Record the date and time of each follow-up call you make, the person you tried to contact, his or her media outlet, the subject, and the outcome. When you enter the outcome information, be detailed so that you can refer to matters that were discussed in subsequent contacts.

Never let your story die. Constantly think ahead and try to plan your next move. I've emphasized that once the media have told your story, they will abandon you and move on. Actively think of ways to keep your story alive and of interest to the media.

While leafing through *Prevention* magazine, Kate Adamson noticed that the magazine was running a Picture of Health Contest and decided to enter. To say the least, her entry was unusual because disabled people rarely enter fitness contests. However, Kate and her husband realized that *Prevention* has 11 million readers and that she had an exceptionally unique slant.

It paid off. Kate became one of five finalists and received extensive media coverage. She scored big because she was creative, stepped out of her comfort zone, and took a risk by entering the contest.

Kate has continued her relationship with *Prevention*. The magazine is having all the contest finalists participate in marathons that it is sponsoring around the country. Although Kate's doctors won't let her run, *Prevention* is flying her to all the race sites, and she will speak at each one. Kate is setting up publicity events for the times she will visit each of the marathon sites.

Action Plan

1. Write a few press release headlines in different styles.

_____

_____

_____

_____

_____

2. Describe how you can be a resource for your media contacts.

_____

_____

_____

_____

_____

3. What information should you have in your media list?

_____

_____

_____

_____

4. Write a script for three follow-up calls to people in the media.

_____

_____

_____

_____

_____

10

BUILD ON YOUR PASSIONS

The secret of success is making your vocation your vacation.
—MARK TWAIN

This chapter will cover:

- Creating passion
- Building with success
- Sustaining passion
- Generating energy
- Self-motivation
- Faking it

GET NOTICED BY FOLLOWING your passion: doing what you love. When you work at what you love, you perform better and enjoy it more. When your passion shines through, you make connections naturally. Your passions make it easy for you to express yourself and influence others. People identify with your passion, and it excites them. They pay close attention and follow you.

When you're excited about what you do, you bounce out of bed each morning because you can't wait to start. You dive right into your work and savor it throughout the day. It makes time fly. Here are some of the things passion can do:

- *Passion attracts.* Passionate people are magnets. People are attracted to those who have deep convictions and strong points of view. They want to learn from them and share their vision. Passionate people are full of light and life; they inspire and excite. Followers line up to support them; they become their apostles and spread the word. They do whatever is needed to help them succeed.
- *Passion motivates.* It helps you sail over hurdles and makes learning a breeze. Passion whets your appetite and feeds your curiosity. It compels you to explore your interests and learn all about them. The more you learn, the more you want to know, and pretty soon you're an expert—and becoming an expert didn't feel like hard work. Other people are drawn to experts; they admire them, want to work with them, and want to have them on their side.
- *Passion unites.* When teams are fueled by passion, a powerful group dynamic occurs. The members' excitement intensifies geometrically, and turns into a mission. Each member becomes a crusader who will fight battles and move mountains to advance the cause. Passionate teams accomplish wonders because they believe that everything is possible and no problem is too great to overcome. They let nothing stand in their way.

Start with your dreams, with things you think about constantly and would like to try. Use them for motivation. Find people with sim-

PULL THE RIGHT STRING

As a child, I was uncomfortably shy, even withdrawn. I always felt that I didn't fit in. When I was 12, I went to a summer camp where

I became involved in a marionette program. In that program we made our own puppets from start to finish. We built their bodies, painted their faces, sewed their clothes, made their shoes, attached their strings, and learned how to make each part move. Then we learned our parts, practiced, and rehearsed until we could perform our roles flawlessly. We worked extremely hard, but it didn't seem difficult because we loved what we were doing.

By immersing myself in this new interest, involving myself with other kids who loved puppets and with whom I performed, I found passion. My passion changed me as a person and brought me out of my shell. In the marionette program we shared a common love that helped us work together; we mastered puppetry and had fun. In the process, we became good puppet makers and puppeteers, and my life was changed forever.

ilar ardor and let your mutual passion be the connecting link. Communicate your enthusiasm to enlist supporters and gain referrals.

WARNING ▶ Passion can have its downside: It can be blinding and carry you away. It can cause you to lose focus and overlook what others plainly see. Excitement can sweep you away, causing you to lose perspective and make mistakes. Passionate people frequently go overboard. Understand and be alert to these dangers. Stay grounded and pay attention to other people's reactions. When others indicate that you're overdoing it or being unrealistic, lower your flame. Their signals may be subtle, so watch closely. Fight the impulse to dismiss their reactions; consider the possibility that they could be correct.

■ ■ ■ Creating Passion

Some people are inherently passionate; by nature they are enthusiastic and optimistic. New ideas and opportunities capture their imagination and excite them. Others are just the opposite. They react skeptically and negatively; these naysayers respond coolly and rarely become impassioned or deeply involved. They sit back and wait to be convinced.

Passion doesn't always hit you with a seismic jolt. Although it can come on suddenly with a bang, it also can build gradually, build cumulatively, and be just as deep. As you work, learn, and become more involved, your enthusiasm can develop. When you master your interests and become acknowledged as an expert, it can take hold. If you stop to take stock, you suddenly may realize that you love what you do, understand how much you have achieved, and become aware of the benefits it provides.

Most people think that passion is always instinctive and beyond their control, but I disagree. Passion can also be learned and increased. Here's how:

- *Surround yourself with active people.* Active people tend to be curious and have a wide range of interests. They are usually open, adventurous, and eager to share. As you spend time with them, their love of involvement will rub off on you. They will introduce you to exciting new areas and encourage you in your quests.

- *Be with interesting people.* Interesting people can introduce you to stimulating new pursuits that you probably would not have discovered on your own. These new directions can energize you and expand your life. They can help you become more positive and adventurous. Interesting people also take interest in and support your pursuits.

- *Spend time with positive people.* Positive people are supportive; they will encourage and help you move forward so that you can achieve your objectives. When problems arise, their support will help you move forward and keep you from becoming discouraged.

- *Eliminate negative people from your life.* Negative people cannot see the light, and so they will try to hold you back.

Their doubts will get the best of them, and they will not provide the encouragement and help you need to succeed. Although it's important to examine everything with a balanced view, constant negativity is demoralizing and eventually will bring you down.

- *Take chances.* Nothing of value comes without risk, and if you hope to succeed, sooner or later you must take chances. Otherwise, you will remain rooted in place while others pass you by. When you take chances, it can add excitement to your life and make it more fun. It can make your successes sweeter and more complete. When you begin taking risks, it can ease your fears and encourage you to take more chances. If some of the risks you take lead to failure, identify your mistakes, learn from them, and try not to repeat them.
- *Enroll in programs.* Attend courses, programs, and activities that push you past your boundaries and help you get unstuck. Do something different; break the mold. I've taken improvisation courses that taught me to respond spontaneously and be completely in the moment. I tried physically challenging programs that put me in dangerous situations and forced me to confront my fears. Avoid being stagnant. Take acting, singing, or dancing lessons. Learn an instrument, ceramics, or a new sport. Constantly push yourself to learn because those who constantly push themselves lead exciting lives.

When you take courses and break your routine, you can meet entirely new groups of people. These individuals can become members of and extend your referral network. They and their contacts can open new dimensions and possibilities for you.

I find that when my life is in balance, I'm more passionate, more excited about my life and work. When I'm more rested and healthier physically, emotionally, and spiritually and not totally swamped with work, I feel everything more. I'm more enthusiastic, energized, and positive. I work hard to maintain a balanced, happy, healthy, and productive life. Balance doesn't just come; you have to plan and work on it.

■ ■ ■ Building with Success

As you develop expertise, your passion can grow. When you succeed, you earn compliments, respect, and acclaim, and that is extremely rewarding. It's also addictive and makes you want more. The fact that others appreciate your accomplishments will encourage you to try harder to retain that standing and surpass your past successes.

When you realize how far you've come, how well you have mastered your interest, it fires you up. As an expert, you can charge more, earn greater respect, attract top customers and clients, and help people more. More people will want to refer their friends and associates to you because they know that you will make them look good. Answering questions, solving problems, and displaying your expertise stimulate you and make you feel great.

I believe the old adage "The more you know, the more you realize how much you don't know." It certainly has been true for me. As I learn more about a subject, I want to know still more, especially when it concerns my clients' businesses. I want to have the answers to every question and find the best, most inventive solutions to the toughest problems. It builds my passion to keep learning and developing greater mastery.

When people recognize your expertise, they can't wait to hear what you have to say. You're invited to speak, give presentations, and appear with the top authorities. You perform on a larger stage. To hold your audiences and be at your best, you become more vocal, dramatic, or colorful. You also work harder to attain more knowledge, and that expands your expertise.

Passion is contagious and is the type of disease you want. When we meet people, we make quick decisions about them; their enthusiasm, excitement, and demeanor influence those decisions. I'm drawn to those who are smiling and relaxed and who seem to have substance: those who are open and welcoming. When I see how much they know and understand, I want to sit, listen, and learn from them. However, when I meet people who look stressed and tired, I walk the other way.

▪ ▪ ▪ Sustaining Passion

Ideas, even the most exciting ones, frequently fizzle out. We've all had brainstorms and epiphanies that eventually fell flat. Initially, they may have fascinated us, but as we got more deeply involved, we discovered fatal flaws. And how many times have we burned out trying to make our great ideas work?

Sustain your passions by getting support. Enlist the help of others, the best people you can find. Start early. Bring the most accomplished experts on board, those who can make the strongest and most inventive contributions so that the process remains fresh and alive. When you work with the best, their ideas, observations, and approaches add spice to the mix and inject it with new life.

If your ideas are flawed, experts usually spot the errors quickly, and that can save you lots of time and effort. They may know of alternatives that could bypass or fix the deficiencies or even strengthen your approach.

Top people, authorities, and thought leaders get it and have broader vision. They will be more likely to understand your ideas, especially those which are new and daring. Accomplished experts may see possibilities where others never even think to look. It's more likely that these authorities will know of and be willing to try new approaches that could make the unlikely work.

Working with the top people teaches and motivates you; it challenges you to do your best and move to a higher level. It may force you to increase your knowledge, improve your performance, and rev up your engine. When you rise to the upper echelons, people notice you, especially the other leaders in your field. They will want to connect with and hang out with you and consider you their peer.

■ ■ ■ Generating Energy

Passion and energy are inexorably connected; they go hand in hand. When you're energized, your passion flows. And when you're lethargic, your passion dips.

We all have foggy, low-energy mornings when it's hard to get out of bed. Respect your rhythm. If you have nothing pressing, stay in bed. Even if it's just for 10 or 15 minutes, it will help you marshal your energy for the rest of the day.

Find ways to boost your energy. How you feel in the morning can impact the rest of your day. As a rule, I tackle the hardest tasks first because as I complete each task, it helps me build momentum that carries me through the day. When I'm lacking energy, I jump-start my day by reading positive, inspiring, get-myself-in-the-mood materials. Or I just reflect. Other people work out, walk, run, listen to music, read the paper, or watch TV. Find what works for you.

Some mornings I feel sluggish and well below speed. On those occasions I give myself a break. I don't immediately try to take on the toughest problems but ease my way in. I perform routine functions such as answering phone calls and correspondence. I prime the pump, clear out the cobwebs, and give myself time to build up to my best.

Some people believe that easing yourself into tasks is simply procrastination. I disagree. I think that our minds never stop; no matter what we do, they constantly are working and organizing, even as we sleep. When you begin your workday by answering e-mail, filing weekly reports, or even playing computer games, your mind will be planning, organizing, and getting up to speed. Then, when you take on tough problems, you will be more focused and more efficient because your mind has warmed up and completed the preliminary steps.

Each day, make a conscious decision to be more passionate, to be a possibility person. When I run into barriers, I stop and think of every alternative, every possible way, and I don't quickly give up. I push myself to examine, explore, and come up with answers and solutions.

▪ ▪ ▪ Self-Motivation

We all have ups and downs. At times you won't feel your usual passion. You can't run your business by your mood; your clients and customers won't put up with it. They want and are entitled to results regardless of how you feel. When you're down, learn to get past it. Find a way to recharge and rebuild your passion.

I reenergize myself by working. When I dive into the issues at hand, my momentum builds, I get lost in my work, and I start moving at full speed. That initial leap can be hard and take some time, but once I start working, I get completely involved.

After a recent speaking engagement in Pittsburgh, disaster struck. My ride to the airport was late. Then we sat in endless gridlock, and it began to pour. The sky literally turned black. When we finally arrived at the terminal, it was 20 minutes before departure. I tried to curbside my luggage and race to the plane.

The redcap told me I was too late, so I asked him to try to get me on board. "Sorry, honey," he said, "If I tried, they would just laugh at me inside." I continued to beg him, but he wouldn't budge.

I asked if the flight might have been delayed, but he just shrugged. Fortunately, another redcap overheard our conversation and volunteered to check. He went into the terminal, and I began calling other airlines for alternative flights, which would have meant going to another terminal, buying a new ticket, and then taking long, circuitous flights home, with all the attendant stress.

About 10 minutes later, the second redcap returned waving two baggage tags. The airport had shut down, he announced; my flight had not departed. I could wait in the lounge and board when flights resumed, which occurred about two hours later.

The second redcap's help and attitude saved my day. He saw the possibilities and checked. Unlike his coworker, he didn't just sit there. He took action and explored the possibilities, and I amply rewarded him. He made it happen; he found a way.

When I travel to speaking engagements, I often arrive late at night and must be up and ready to address an audience early the next morning. Frequently, when I wake up, I'm sluggish, but I know that I have to get ready to appear before a room full of strangers and get them to listen, learn, and enjoy. That's my job.

So I do it; I push myself. I don't apologize or make excuses. I raise my energy level and do my best. As I begin speaking and see the audience members respond, we invariably form a connection. I know that they are listening and absorbing, and I hit my stride. My energy builds, my passion soars, and the audience energizes me. I put all of myself into my presentation, and the audience responds; we connect, form a bond.

■ ■ ■ Faking It

Passion can be faked, at least initially. Actors and salespeople do it constantly. Salespeople are taught to respond to the question "How is business?" by always saying, "It's booming, fabulous, never better"—even though that may not be true.

Be an actor, play a role, and become the part. If you project being passionate, you can get lost in the role and become passionate.

When you're not at your best and your energy is low, put on the best possible face to break the gloom. Act the part of the happy, passionate person, and before you know it, you just may be. By acting passionately, you may get your energy back and move forward at full steam.

Whenever I'm asked the question "How are you?" I always say, "Great!" Regardless of what is happening in my life, I state it heartily, with conviction. The truth is that even during the worst times my life is great. And even when it is comparatively bad for me, it's so much better than so many other people's lives that I definitely have no grounds for complaint.

When people ask how you are and you tell them about your problems, you will scare them away. Lois was so tired of hearing Evelyn's complaints when she greeted her each morning that she stopped saying, "How are you?" Now she only says, "Beautiful day today," smiles, and keeps walking.

If you need to speak about your problems, do so with only your closest friends, confidants, and therapists. Don't spill your problems to the world. If you do, they will notice you for the wrong reasons and steer clear of you.

Don't fake your uniqueness, T. Harv Eker warns. "If you fake your uniqueness, it won't last. You will always feel like a sham because its not who you are. People will see that you're not being authentic."

Action Plan

1. List five ways in which you can learn to identify or increase your passion.

   _____

   _____

   _____

   _____

   _____

2. How can you sustain your passion?

   _____

   _____

   _____

   _____

3. What is a possibility person, and how can you see more possibilities?

   _____

   _____

   _____

   _____

4. Why can it be beneficial to pretend that you feel passionately?

   _____

   _____

   _____

   _____

11

Focus, Focus, Focus

This chapter covers:

- Defining your focus
- Scheduling
- Solving problems
- Sharpening your focus
- Writing

WE CAN'T DO EVERYTHING and certainly can't do it all at once, but some people think they can. They may be impatient and impetuous and fall in love with every new idea. These folks juggle a million and one projects, and most, if not all, of them fail. Therefore, they become frustrated, dejected, and depressed. After a while, they may be reluctant to try anything. They go into a shell.

"Creative thinkers, especially entrepreneurs, have a tendency to take on more and more," Kym Yancey, cofounder and president of eWomenNetwork, observes. "That's the creative disease. They frequently don't examine all of their alternatives and determine the ones that are most important to them."

Clients come to me brimming with ideas. They're bursting with excitement and frequently want to do them all at once. "I have at least five books in me," they announce. Then they want to make movies, give lectures, teach workshops, and build solar-powered submarines. When they try to tell me the details, we all get confused.

As a part of my business, I've always created products: videos, audios, courses, and books—but never all at once. My policy is to produce only one new product per quarter at the most. Sometimes I even skip a few quarters. Spacing my projects allows me to focus on the venture in process and do it right.

Doing it right is critical because you may not get another opportunity. If you provide poor goods or services, you may never get a chance to produce similar items again. People will remember your failure, label you, and be reluctant to buy from you again. When you fail, many people no longer will be willing to help you.

My business consists of three primary parts: speaking (including my crash course on publicity), consulting, and producing and marketing products. At times, my focus shifts so that I concentrate more on one part than on the others. For example, as I write this book, which will be a product, it's my primary focus.

I've structured my business so that all the parts relate, are complementary, and feed each other. When I focus on speaking, my presentations improve. If I perform well, my products sell briskly and I'm hired to do consultations and speak.

People prefer to do business with specialists: those who consistently provide the same goods and services expertly. Most people, especially in business-to-business relationships, do not trust jacks-of-all-trades because they usually don't do everything well.

"Focus is harder to maintain today because so many things are in our environment that distract us," Tommy Newberry believes. "If you're not constantly reminding yourself what your priorities are, you are more susceptible to being distracted and going off track."

▪ ▪ ▪ Defining Your Focus

Focus is the art of doing the following things:

1. Constantly being aware of your goal
2. Deciding what you must do to accomplish it
3. Working to achieve it

Focusing means keeping your eye on the target, concentrating on your main objective. In archery, darts, and other target-based sports, you must focus on the bull's-eye continuously to rack up the highest score. You can't look aimlessly and let your arrows fly anywhere. You must aim for your goal steadily.

Well, businesses must operate similarly. Busy people easily can get sidetracked. They have so much on their plates, so many demands, that they can get diverted and thrown off course. When they spend their time and energy on less important items, the essential tasks may not be completed satisfactorily.

"A lot of businesses fail because people lose their focus," Jay Conrad Levinson explains. "They're easily distracted, and they think that they're supposed to diversify. So they venture away from their expertise and try to get into new areas where they have no expertise and are over their heads. Instead, they should focus on increasing the excellence that brought them success," Levinson maintains. "If you keep your focus and improve your core business, it will help you stand out. Build on your expertise and push forward in the areas you know or those that are within range of it."

Define your focus. Identify the areas that are most important to you and determine how you should apply your time. Don't just look at your business interests; reflect on all the important aspects of your life because they all involve and relate to one another.

Les Hewitt, author of the best-selling *Power of Focus* series of books, teaches that you should select your goals in seven areas:

1. Financial
2. Business

3. Fun time
4. Health
5. Relationships
6. Personal
7. Contributions

Look at each of these items. Where do you stand? Are you moving in the right direction? If you are not, find out how you can get back on track and get to it.

■ ■ ■ Scheduling

When we work, something or other always pops up that can throw us off, and it usually takes forever to resolve. As a result, we may not spend our time efficiently. Things that should have been tackled are not, and before we know it, we're way behind.

Mark LeBlanc has a fabulous method for avoiding this problem and increasing your focus. He recommends that you write your financial goals for the month and then, below it, list three specific actions that you will take that day to reach those goals.

I've adopted Mark's system of setting monthly and daily goals with wonderful results. Here's how it works.

- On the first day of the month, I set my monthly income goal. I try to be realistic by setting a figure I can reach, but I also try to push myself to be more productive.
- Each workday, first thing in the morning, I write on a separate sheet my monthly financial goal and three actions that I will take to reach it. Listing my monthly goal reminds me daily how much I want to earn and keeps me focused on my objective. Setting three daily goals keeps me focused on hitting my targets.

    Each of the three daily actions must be quantifiable by (1) the time it will take and (2) money it will generate. Activities could include calling an associate to discuss a referral, making marketing calls, cleaning my office, and sending out invitations to my next teleconference.

The three activities become the basis of my daily schedule. Writing them helps me think about my day, set priorities, organize my time, and decide how I want to proceed.

- I also list my daily personal, health, and relaxation goals. Since speaking publicly is a major part of my business, I travel extensively, and that can be stressful and physically and mentally exhausting. Therefore, I must keep my body and mind in good shape to be at my best for business and for myself.
- Throughout the day, I check my list to keep myself on schedule. Each day, I ask myself two questions, which Mark calls the AM and PM questions.
  - The AM question is, "What three things will I do today to meet my monthly revenue goals?"
  - At the end of the day, when I stop working, I ask the PM question: "Did I do the three things I listed to meet my monthly revenue goals?" I simply check off the PM question with a yes or a no without comments or judgments. I focus on results. If I do all three items every day that month, I will hit my monthly revenue goals.

The PM question lets me review my day and see well my time was spent. I learn if my work advanced my financial goals and what more I need to accomplish. Then I can make the necessary adjustments or set additional goals.

Recently, I've set aside one full day a week to do nothing involved with work. This means no business appointments, no phone calls, no e-mail, and no talking about work. I have learned that I need a complete break to relax, reenergize, and change my mind's focus.

As a part of that change, I've also started setting leisure-day goals. I may plan to take a hike, read a book, or just relax on the deck. Although my leisure-time goals are looser and more flexible than my business goals, setting them has kept me from slipping into work-related activities on my days off.

I also schedule my weekly health routine. I set targets for and measure my diet, plan my exercises, and even set aside 10 minutes of silence. Then, at the end of each month, I examine how many of my objectives I achieved and where I need to improve. Attending to my health and state of mind enables me to be at my best for my business and my clients.

When I work systematically and meet my goals, it motivates me and increases my drive. When I accomplish each task, my energy and my passion build. I get in the zone and feel that I can achieve anything.

Each week, I reflect for 30 minutes on my business. Les Hewitt suggests that you reflect for an hour, but I find that 30 minutes works well for me.

■ ■ ■ Solving Problems

If you're in business, people want you or your products to solve their problems; that's the bottom line. They have a problem they need you to fix.

Many businesses fail because they don't solve their customers' problems. They lose sight of what their customers want. In the past, businesses could get away with selling customers what they had and not worry about what the customers wanted. Customers were expected to conform their operations to the products available or incur the cost of having them adapted or custom-made.

That's no longer the case today. With new developments in technology and increased competition, customers want goods that will provide what they need. They want items that will solve their problems. If you can't deliver what they need, they will turn to someone who can. Customers want and are entitled to receive results, and that usually means having their problems solved.

When your clients or customers have problems, learn whether the issues are industrywide. If they are, examine the various solutions that may have been tried. One of them or a version of it may be exactly what you need to solve your client's dilemma.

Then determine how the problem is affecting your client and the specific harm it has caused. To solve problems, you must understand them and all their implications. Otherwise you're just guessing, and that increases the risks.

Mary Jane, a nurse, invented a product that decreases the spread of germs. She realized that when people have colds, they toss their used tissues in the trash, spreading germs. When trash is emptied, especially in public places, people are exposed to the germs and can spread them farther. Mary Jane developed a product that safely disposes of used tissues.

Instead of focusing on her product and how it worked, I created a publicity campaign for Mary Jane that stressed the problems that germs and spreading germs create. We knew that when people became aware of the problem, they would want a product that could solve it, which Mary Jane's invention did.

Figure out what your customers want and how you can solve their problems. If you can't help them, refer them to someone who can.

Timmy drives an airport shuttle bus. All day he jockeys passengers between the airport and his company's parking lot. He picks them up, helps them get their luggage in and out of the van, hands out slips listing their parking place numbers, and drops them off. It's a repetitive and frequently difficult job because some people's luggage weighs a ton.

Timmy greets passengers with a big, warm smile as if he's delighted to see them. "Let me get that. You just go in the van and relax," he says as he bounds out of the van and hoists their luggage on the rack. He's always cheerful and friendly and helps passengers feel at ease. He truly seems to love his job and does it excellently.

Are you willing to help? Timmy is always focused and out front. He knows his job and has figured out how he can give the most help. He does it with a smile and does it well.

◼ ◼ ◼ Sharpening Your Focus

Make your focus laser-sharp. Identify your most important and most immediate objectives. Then break them down into small, achievable steps and zero in on how you can accomplish each step. Clear your deck by putting less important matters on the back burner.

The sharper and more precise your focus is, the more successful you will be. Specialize and develop expertise. When you demonstrate that you can provide expert goods or services, customers and clients will vie to do business with you.

Today people are taught to generate multiple streams of revenue, and that can lead them astray. Moving into other areas can take you away from your core business and place you in new and unfamiliar terrain. If you move into new areas, get expert help and don't neglect your core business.

Limit your areas of focus; never have more than three. Be clear on your planning and strategies and enlist expert help.

For years, I was solicited to sell various products at my speaking engagements. Other speakers had done so successfully, so I thought I would give it a whirl. Although I sold products that I used and liked, it didn't work out. Trying to sell other items diverted me from my core business and diluted my focus. I had too much on my plate, so I stopped marketing those products.

I'm an expert publicity strategist, but I'm not an expert in advertising. I don't know much about branding or marketing. Therefore, I send my clients to referral partners who are advertising, branding, or marketing experts. In turn, I get referrals from them.

Kym Yancey advocates the Final Four approach. He advises people to write a two-column list of all their alternatives, everything they have to do. "Then compare all of the items on the list two at a time to see which is more important. Then keep going until you whittle through the entire list. When you determine which alternative is most important to you, laser your focus on it," he suggests.

■ ■ ■ **CONNECTING LINK** ■ ■ ■

To sharpen my focus, I take workshops that help me improve my speaking or bolster areas that I need to improve. For example, I recently took a course on how to sell better from the stage.

Study with people who are the best: experts in their fields. When you work with the best, it helps you look and become better. The top experts tend to attract the most promising students. Since you have a common interest, some of those students can become your network partners.

When you take courses and workshops, connect with the leaders and instructors. They have the best connections and can hook you up with them. Often, they're allied with organizations that also could help advance your career.

■ ■ ■ Writing

Test your ideas and approaches in writing. If you can't explain them clearly, you may not have thought them through, don't understand them sufficiently, or are not convinced of their value. Also, your focus could be off. If you can't express your thoughts on paper, you won't be able to explain them verbally to others, and so you may not be able to attract the support you need to succeed.

Some people excel at verbally selling weak ideas. Their charisma and personality overcome holes in their proposals.

These charmers primarily convince and entertain rather than present solid facts. They give salespeople a bad name, and their tactics usually don't work over the long term.

Your focus should be to build and maintain close long-term relationships, to give people information that will let them decide for themselves. Sales that are based on charming people or talking them into what they may not believe or what may be less than completely truthful usually leads to one-shot deals.

People are busy. They want written proposals they can read when they have the chance. State your ideas clearly and concisely in an e-mail that runs less than a half screen. Carefully read and recheck the e-mail before sending it to make sure it's error-free.

Putting your ideas in writing grounds your thinking. It sharpens your focus by making you go through logical, step-by-step progressions to explain clearly how your concept will work. As you write, flaws in theories become apparent, especially when you try to describe or give examples of how they should be applied.

Even if you have an exceptional memory, write lists. Consider it an exercise to help you clarify and focus your thoughts. Don't be afraid to refer to your notes at meetings or appointments. Periodically checking them will keep you focused and on track. It also will show that you're prepared, precise, and professional. Checking your notes is preferable to forgetting important items.

Action Plan

1. Define focus.

_____

_____

_____

_____

_____

2. How can you use Mark LeBlanc's goal-setting system in your business?

_____

_____

_____

_____

_____

3. Describe how you can sharpen your focus.

_____

_____

_____

_____

4. Express three of your ideas or approaches in writing.

_____

_____

_____

_____

_____

_____

12

Always Keep It Real

This chapter covers:

- Expecting changes
- Learning what they want
- Past customers
- Reviving old business
- Vendors
- Consulting

IT'S EASY TO GET LOST in your work, to become so involved that you lose contact with your customers or clients or go off on tangents. When you work on a project, you may take an idea and develop it brilliantly, but when you present it, you find that it's not what the client wanted. You get noticed, but for the wrong reasons.

Minimize the possibility of going astray by understanding completely what your clients want. At the beginning of every project, clarify their objectives and the courses they wish to take. When projects are under way, constantly stay in contact with your clients. Create clear lines of communication and keep them open by doing the following:

- Frequently update your clients.
- Tell your clients what you've done so far.
- Inform your clients of your plans and time lines.
- Solicit your clients' input and feedback.
- Involve your clients more deeply; encourage them to participate more personally in their projects.

■ ■ ■ Expecting Changes

Problems arise and unforeseen events occur that influence or radically alter projects, and they frequently take place at the worst possible times. Regardless of how well you plan, changes will occur and you will be forced to deal with them. It's how well you handle those changes that will distinguish you.

Learn to juggle. When disasters strike, immediately attend to them; put all fires out. Get the situation under control but continue to keep the project on track.

After we had been working together for several weeks, a client called me and said, "I don't love the direction our work together has taken. I need help from you in other ways." I was shocked. I felt that our work was right on track. However, it was obvious that my client had given the matter a lot of thought and wanted change, and so I listened to her explain her reasons and outline her needs. Then we clarified exactly what she wanted and changed course.

If we had not established good communications, my client would not have contacted me to express her feelings. I could not have delivered what she needed, and she would have been disappointed. Fortunately, we caught the problem in time and were able to complete the project successfully. Since then, we have worked together on several matters. Before beginning each project, I made sure we clarified our plans and objectives, and I'm happy to say that the projects turned out exceptionally well.

Some customers and clients are plain difficult. Many are hard-driving, strong-willed dynamos who built success through the strength of their personalities. Usually they are demanding, uncompromising individuals who insist on playing by their rules. Others may be difficult because they constantly change their minds, worry all the time, micromanage, or are impossible to please. It's hard to establish a dialog with these clients; it's hard to complete your plans.

> ■ ■ ■ **CONNECTING LINK** ■ ■ ■
>
> If you can't communicate with your customers or clients, seriously consider whether you should be working together. When you can't communicate, your projects will be plagued with problems and those problems will affect your personal life. When you can't communicate, it's a bad match. Face the facts, avoid further pain, and move on.

Problems are inherent in business; they come with the territory. Take frequent reality checks so that you can spot trouble quickly and deal with it. I like to conduct short surveys by asking four or five sharply focused questions that can be answered in a minute or less.

■ ■ ■ Learning What They Want

E-mail your customers short surveys. Even if they don't respond, they will notice your efforts. If they respond, which some will, their answers can be helpful.

Don't barrage your clients with surveys. Send them only at these times:

1. While you're working on their projects
2. When the project has been completed

Survey to learn your customers' feelings about your overall performance, not to inquire about the specifics of how the work is being done or should be done. If those matters should be discussed in greater detail, do so directly with the client, not in a survey.

Many businesspeople don't survey their customers and clients because they don't want to know the answers. They have no interest in keeping it real and serving their patrons' needs.

Business operators who don't want to know what their customers or clients honestly think are relics of an era that no longer exists; they are operating under yesterday's outmoded rules. Businesses that don't understand and satisfy their clients' needs cannot survive in the current business environment.

In the subject line of your e-mail, refer to your survey as "1-Minute Survey" to let the recipients immediately know that it is brief. Make the survey and all the questions short and directly to the point. People resent long surveys and frequently won't bother to read, much less answer, them.

When you review survey responses, make note of the answers that indicate problems with your goods or services that should be dealt with. Keep copies of all replies for your records. If a response alerts you to a pressing problem, immediately call the customer or client, discuss the issue, and make arrangements to solve it.

In your e-mail, write a brief sentence or two explaining why you are sending the survey. Then ask the survey questions. Here is an example:

Dear _____:

To help us make sure that our service is providing exactly what you need, please answer the short survey below and e-mail it back to us. Thank you for your help!

1. Are you satisfied with our service?
2. How can we serve you better?

3. What do you like best about our service?
4. What do you like least about our service?
5. How can we improve?

Encourage responses by providing incentives for those who answer and return the survey. As incentives, you could offer a discount coupon for a product or service, articles, reports, resource listings, or other information. When you offer free or discounted goods or services to recipients' friends, it can attract new customers.

When you write your survey questions, resist the urge to add more questions. If you feel it is important to get other information from your customers or clients, contact them directly and ask.

"Almost everything we provide is based on what people have told us, not on what we thought of ourselves," Craig Newmark notes. In 2000 Craigslist had to decide who it should charge to post items on its site. Newmark and his staff talked with lots of people, and the consensus was that they should charge those who were paying other businesses more money to provide less effective ads. Now Craigslist charges only real estate agents, apartment brokers, and job posters such as recruiters and employers. All other postings, which make up the vast majority of Craigslist's postings, are free.

■ ■ ■ Past Customers

Survey your former clients and customers. Sending brief e-mail surveys to inactive clients and customers will remind them about you. If they had a favorable experience with you, jogging their memories may spur them to recommend you to others or work with you again.

Contact your former clients and customers within a year of the completion of your last project together. If you developed a good relationship or worked together closely, consider adding a personal note to your e-mail. Here's an example:

Dear Tom:

I hope this finds you, Betty, and the boys well and your business thriving!

Please take a minute to answer this short survey and return your answers to me. I would really appreciate it.

Thanks,

Jill

1. Were you satisfied with our service?
2. How could we have served you better?
3. What did you like best about our service?
4. What did you like least about our service?
5. How can we improve?

■ ■ ■ Reviving Old Business

Business guru Jim White, the CEO of JL White International and author of *What's My Purpose* (JL White International, 2007), recommends that his clients survey their former customers. When a former customer states how Jim's client—lets call it Corporation X—could have served it better, what it liked least about Corporation X's service, or how Corporation X could improve, Jim instructs Corporation X to address and fix those problems immediately.

When Corporation X has put the remedies in place, Jim has it go back to its ex-customer and say, "Thanks for your feedback. Your advice was right on point and let us show you exactly what we have done as a direct result of it."

Corporation X's former customers often are impressed and proceed to give Corporation X business. If a customer does this, Corporation X asks that customer for a testimonial stating that it worked with Corporation X, a problem arose, but when Corporation

X learned of the problem, it promptly fixed it. Now they are working together again with excellent results.

Corporation X will show the testimonial to potential customers because it illustrates that Corporation X is human, makes mistakes, but moves promptly to fix them. The testimonial also shows that Corporation X is customer-oriented and skilled at problem solving, and that helps it land new business.

■ ■ ■ Vendors

Vendors are pivotal figures. Since they serve a number of businesses, they can be a major source of information and referrals. In their industries, venders know all the players. They see who is good and who is not, company problems, and personnel shifts. Vendors understand how the industry works: its trends, problems, and innovations. They know who may be looking for work, who excels at certain tasks, and who might need your help.

Bill sells paint products to auto body repair shops in northern Virginia. He personally calls on his customers, and so he sees the quality of work they turn out. Bill knows which shops buy his premium lines and which use poorer-quality paint. As an industry insider, Bill is privy to the rumor mill. Thus, he knows which shops have financial troubles, receive lots of customer complaints, and face heavy employee turnover. He knows when a talented employee may be unhappy and looking to move.

Friends and friends of friends constantly ask Bill to recommend body shops. Bill only sends them to the finest; the shops that he knows consistently do an outstanding job. Bill's customers also call him when they are looking to hire new employees.

Look to your vendors. Each of your vendors could be an excellent referral source. Don't wait for them to send you referrals voluntarily;

take the initiative and contact them. Explain that you're looking to increase your business. Ask what they think you should do. Find out how they think you could produce the most outstanding work and improve your business.

In exchange for their help, vendors may try to sell you their products or get you to boost your purchases of what you already buy. If they sell top products, buying more could be a smart trade-off because vendors tend to be a fabulous source of information and referrals.

■ ■ ■ **CONNECTING LINK** ■ ■ ■

Many of the vendors that supply my business are my referral partners. They include writers, printers, designers, and computer experts, to name just a few. Identify vendors that could be strong referral partners and contact them.

At my speaking engagements, I sell Mem-Cards, which are learning aids that contain information from my books. The company that supplies me exhibits at many trade shows, and at its booth it displays my Mem-Cards. When potential customers go to its booth and look at my Mem-Cards, the vendor talks me up, telling them that if they ever need a great speaker, they should think of me. The vendor explains how to use the cards and how much they can help. Its efforts have brought me a great number of speaking engagements.

Think about how every one of your vendors could refer business to you. Know what you want of them. Then, when you see them, specifically ask, "Do you know anyone who could use a publicist, a Web site designer, or an exciting public speaker?" You may be surprised at how many will answer in the affirmative.

■ ■ ■ Consulting

If you have expertise, leverage that knowledge by becoming a consultant. As a consultant, you can advise people in your field who need your particular expertise or those in other businesses who want specific advice. Find out who might need help in your specialty and contact them.

Practitioners make the best consultants because they have hands-on experience. They have been in the trenches, have faced and solved the problems, and know how the industry works. Practitioners are focused on providing practical, concrete solutions that work, not just theories or vague ideas.

My peers and competitors frequently hire me as a consultant. Other publicists call and say, "Jill, I have this client. I don't know what to do." Then they explain the problem, we discuss it, and I tell them what to do. We may have just one consulting session, or I may consult with them throughout the project.

A marketing firm may need advice on how to handle a problem for a campaign that is similar to one that I previously ran. They will hire me to advise them on specific issues. I also have been hired by businesses to consult with their in-house employees while they are running publicity campaigns.

Members of various firms have taken my crash course in publicity and become my clients. A number have hired me to advise them on how to serve their clients. Usually they take my advice, go back to the client, and sound like a hero.

An advantage of offering consulting services is that satisfied clients frequently give me additional business. Many find it a bargain to pay me a single fee and get my advice before they get involved in projects and campaigns. I enjoy consulting because it brings me an interesting variety of work that doesn't tie me up extensively.

My consulting clients also have been excellent referral sources who have sent me lots of new work. In addition, consultations can provide wonderful breaks; they can let you work on interesting matters that differ from your usual routine. For example, I know busy physicians, architects, and contractors who consult on legal matters occasionally to do something different.

Action Plan

1. How can you maintain clear lines of communication with your clients and customers?

_____

_____

_____

_____

2. What questions should you include in client or customer surveys?

_____

_____

_____

_____

_____

_____

3. How does Jim White's method of reviving past business work?

_____

_____

_____

_____

4. Which of your vendors could be significant sources of referral or information for you?

_____

_____

_____

13

Balancing It Out

This chapter covers:

- Generosity
- Giving it away
- Overdoing
- Specializing
- Emotions

BUSINESS IS NOT ALWAYS about money, although for most people the bottom line influences a lot of their decisions. In business, profits are always a consideration; they are the measuring rod. But sometimes the best way to get noticed is by forgoing some profits, charging a bit less, giving a little more—balancing it out.

While I was working on a consulting project with an old client, she was having severe money issues. Since she had to keep her expenses down, she asked to borrow my media list for a promotion for her business. Bear in mind that I never lend my media list. That list is crucial to my business; I've been compiling and refining it for years. It's tightly organized, contains contact and other information for thousands of sources, and is irreplaceable to me.

I decided to lend my list to that client, but I told her when I needed it back, stressed its importance to me, and crossed my fingers. I went out on a limb because I liked her and knew she really needed my help. It might not have been a good risk, and it may never pay off for me, but when I examined all the considerations, I decided that it was the right thing for me to do.

It all ended well. My client returned the list and told me that it really helped her. Best of all, she realized that I went out on a limb for her and was truly grateful. That gave me a great sense of satisfaction and helped cement our relationship.

Generosity

I believe in giving; it's a central part of my life. Helping others is rewarding and makes me feel good. Few things are as satisfying to me as the looks of gratitude I receive when I help. Giving is a way to say thanks for my good fortune and all that I've received. It's a way to pass the torch.

For me, giving is good business. It's helped me forge close relationships with many wonderful people. Friendships are important to me. I want my clients to think of me as someone who really wants to help, someone who cares, not just a hired gun.

I don't give to be noticed, but it sure has done the trick. The people I've helped always express their appreciation and have gone out of their way to help me. Also, they continually refer new business to me. With some of these individuals, I've built lifelong bonds and they've become dear friends.

When I give, I try to give generously, fully, and without expecting anything in return. I try to incorporate giving in both my business and my personal life. When I give in my business, I consider many factors: who I'm dealing with, their needs and circumstances, our relationship, and how much I can and want to give at that time.

Most of my giving is small, but I do it frequently, and it cumulatively mounts up. When my schedule allows, I'm happy to give my time. If I have a 30-minute telephone consultation and we cover everything in half that time, I may charge only half my fee or not charge at all. If a caller needs additional time, I often throw it in. I also give when I think it will help someone succeed.

Colonel Greg Cook, a consultant to the Pentagon and a military insider, enrolled in my 90-day program to learn how to create and run a publicity campaign. However, his heavy consulting schedule created delays and prevented him from completing some key assignments.

When Colonel Cook completed the program, I was reluctant to let him embark on his campaign because I wasn't convinced he could get the results that he wanted. I gave him additional one-on-one instruction at no cost to make sure he was fully prepared to create and run a successful campaign.

Don't be cheap. "People can be cheap," according to Mimi Donaldson. "I bring a bunch of books to networking events and give them out. I don't sell them. When you give your goods to others, they help market them for you. They tell their friends and associates; they recommend you and your products. Many speakers don't give their books away. By not giving a book that probably cost them less than $10, they could take themselves out of the running for a much higher-paying speaking engagement. Think of your goods as brochures, selling tools, and give them away," Donaldson advises.

A number of years ago I became the companion of Camille, an 80-year-old woman, through the group Senior Companion. I signed up to spend an hour a week with Camille, but it soon became two to three weekly visits that occupied well over 10 hours of my time. And it lasted for over five years, until Camille died.

Camille became family and deeply affected my life. I took her to movies and the theater and ran errands for her. We dined together and just hung out; she became a dear friend. During a theater performance, Camille had a heart attack and I rushed her to the hospital, and that actually saved her life.

My relationship with Camille was profiled in *Woman's Day* magazine in a feature called "Acts of Kindness, Angels on Earth." When I began my relationship with Camille, receiving publicity for it never entered my mind. Initially, when *Woman's Day* contacted me, I was reluctant to become involved. However, Camille felt an article describing our relationship could provide a powerful example for others.

When the article ran, my phone rang incessantly; everyone wanted to talk. Of all the publicity I've received, the accolades, the thanks, none have been as rewarding as the *Woman's Day* article. Spending time with Camille was a gift, and the article is a cherished memory.

Giving It Away

Many business experts instruct people to give their goods and services freely to drum up business. They tell them to give sample products or free service sessions. Giving goods and services, the experts believe, will generate interest and build demand for their clients' wares.

I'm reluctant to give freebies because it's hard to measure the return. If 80 percent of those who get free items will become your clients or customers, give, give, give! However, a smaller return may not make good business sense. Let me explain.

If you offer a 30-minute free telephone consultation, it could monopolize your time and take you away from billable or more promising work. Just ten 30-minute calls add up to at least five hours on the phone. Phone consultations take total concentration and can be intense, exhaust you, and drain the life out of the rest of your day.

Some people need to come out on top in every transaction. With them it's a contest they have to win. These people will push you to lower your price, do more work, use more expensive materials, and give them a better deal. Although they want you to give, give, give, they rarely are willing to reciprocate. They don't want to strike a fair deal; they just want to win.

When I sense that I'm dealing with such people, I pull away. Even if I give them everything they want, they eventually will want more. To me, their business is not worth the aggravation.

If you offer to give samples, limit the size of the gift. Offer 10- or 15-minute free consultations or propose that the first half-hour session be at a reduced price. Try to give enough to create interest without breaking the bank.

With prospective clients, I conduct an introductory free 15-minute intake call. I prefer not to meet prospects personally; I want to screen them on the phone first. In most cases I can answer their questions, determine their needs, and get a feel for them and their problems in a 10- to 15-minute session. If during a call I feel that we need more time, I usually let the call continue or reschedule it for when I have more time.

As an author and speaker, I follow Jay Conrad Levinson's advice: "Say 'yes' to every request for an interview or to write a blurb for a book. Always sign autographs, especially in your books. Consider it goodwill to help maintain your popularity."

■ ■ ■ Overdoing

Experts also advise business operators to give lavishly in order to get noticed. Some recommend that they build their businesses by showering patrons with service, going overboard, and making a big splash. I call this the avalanche approach.

I believe in giving more than your client or customer expects but not in going overboard. Always do the best job possible and provide something more than you're obligated to give, but don't go wild. When you're starting in business, you may have to extend yourself to open those initial doors. However, continuously overdoing is rarely cost-effective in light of the effort you must make.

Like an avalanche, going overboard can set loose forces you can't contain. It can overwhelm you and set a standard that is difficult or impossible to keep meeting. If you begin a relationship by giving so much, your clients or customers will expect you to continue providing at that level. If your efforts fall below that standard even once, they will notice and may feel shortchanged, feel that they're not getting their money's worth. Your entire relationship could change.

■ ■ ■ **CONNECTING LINK** ■ ■ ■

If you choose to give abundantly, give to charities, nonprofit organizations, or the needy. Help your clients and customers when you can but remember that they are not charities.

Some of the ways I give are providing free consulting service for nonprofit and community organizations. Each time I give my crash course in publicity, I reserve a seat for a person who really needs it but can't afford the fee.

Give your customers and clients what they need and then put a cherry on top. However, don't throw in an entire additional cake. Charge them fairly for the work they receive. Be generous but professional.

■ ■ ■ Specializing

As you build your business, watch out for a common trap that usually works like this. When you demonstrate your excellence, customers and clients come to you because you are a proven quantity who consistently provides great results. When they know that your service is outstanding or that your product really works, your patrons recommend you and your reputation spreads.

Before long, you become a specialist and are acknowledged for your great expertise. Clients and customers beat down your door. You attract bigger, better, higher-paying clients and can charge more. You become an admired brand, and your business expands. But specialization can be a double-edged sword.

When you specialize and money pours in, you can get stuck. Everyone wants to hire you to do the same work. Except for a few minor changes, the bulk of your work is repetitive and you're not exposed to much that's different or new. Without variety, your vision can narrow; you may not be challenged and forced to learn.

Although we learn through repetition, repetition can kill. First, it can make you comfortable and complacent. You like what you're doing, it becomes easy, and you love the rewards. After a while, the repetition can get to you. You miss the excitement, the variety, and the challenges, but you can't risk killing the golden goose. You continue to do the same old thing with few or no breaks. Pretty soon boredom sets in; you get grumpy and grouchy and hate your work.

Follow the advice of financial experts. They tell investors to build portfolios balanced with stocks, bonds, real estate, and other investments. Branch out, diversify, and add other dimensions to your work.

■ ■ ■ Emotions

Business doesn't always run smoothly. People may become impatient, frustrated, and even incensed. Business pressures or personal or family problems can heighten their emotions and cause them to unload on you. Emotional reactions can destroy relationships, even ones that have been close for years.

As an emotional person, I understand their feelings: their desire to be successful, their anxiety, and their fear of disappointment. I've been deeply upset when promising opportunities collapsed and totally frustrated when I had to wait endlessly while simple matters went unresolved. It can be maddening.

Because of my emotional nature, I have had to learn how to handle highly charged people and situations. When someone is highly critical, judgmental, or cross, I pull back and then tighten the reins. I let the other person speak without interrupting, even to defend myself. I take notes, and when he or she has said it all, I take control.

Calmly and unemotionally I address their concerns, but I do not address their opinions. I take the emotions out of the conversation and focus it entirely on our business. I present the facts and tell them what I noticed, not what I feel.

When emotions are involved, I never deal with them in e-mails or written communications. E-mail can intensify problems because it tends to make communiqués read more harshly than intended. Many people zip off e-mails and subsequently realize that they should never have been sent.

If a situation has become emotional, pick up the phone and try to deal with it as soon as possible. Nip it in the bud. If you can talk on a one-to-one human basis, your conflicts usually can be resolved. The first few exchanges may be awkward, but let the other person speak and listen to what he or she says. Try to control your feelings, to be understanding and accommodating.

■ ■ ■ **CONNECTING LINK** ■ ■ ■

If all your eggs are in one basket, you're taking a huge risk. Business goes in cycles, so make sure you are protected because your markets could change quickly and even disappear. Recently, this happened to people who focused their entire businesses on real estate. When the market fell, they were burned.

When your business is doing well, examine where you stand. If all your income comes from one source, think how you could diversify. Investigate ways to add new opportunities, inject more challenges, and go in new directions. Don't throw away what you have but look around. See what might capture your interest and become a good business venture. Explore adding other dimensions that would stimulate your business and you.

When you move in a new direction, don't go too far afield. Build upon and don't abandon your core business. Stay connected to what you know or can learn easily.

As I've mentioned, some people are simply unreasonable and uncompromising. If they strike out at you emotionally, get out before they become abusive. Take your losses, soothe your wounds, and cut them loose. Tomorrow will be much brighter!

Action Plan

1. What samples can you give to get more business?

_____

_____

_____

2. In your business, what would be the right amount to give and what would amount to going overboard?

_____

_____

_____

_____

_____

3. What is the major danger of specializing, and how you can address it?

_____

_____

_____

_____

_____

4. How should you deal with emotional contacts by clients and customers?

_____

_____

_____

_____

_____

14

Service Makes a Difference

This chapter covers:

- Ten Commandments of Business
- Acting pleasantly
- Responding
- Heart-centered marketing
- Encouraging
- Blaming

GET NOTICED BY SATISFYING your customers and clients. Find out what they want and then deliver it—every time. Consistently provide outstanding products and service.

Customers want and deserve results. They expect what they were promised, what they paid for; they expect it to work well and last. Anything less will disappoint or even anger them, and they probably will stop doing business with you. To create and keep satisfied customers, constantly perform as advertised or better. If you do, your customers will stick with you. They will sing your praises, tell their friends and neighbors about you, and help build your brand.

"Treat everyone like you want to be treated," advises Craig Newmark, the founder of Craigslist. "Give people a break and act in good conscience." To Newmark, who built Craigslist from a simple events list to the seventh most frequently visited site on the Internet, "giving people a break means helping people out and giving them the benefit of the doubt. It also means following through with really good customer service, the best we can do."

Many businesses make the mistake of trying to sell their customers what they have instead of providing what their customers need. Make satisfying your customers your top priority and structure your business on the basis of that objective. When you consistently satisfy customers, they will be appreciative and loyal and your business will thrive.

■ ■ ■ Ten Commandments of Business

One of the best ways to satisfy customers and clients is by creating a business that gives them what they want at a fair price and always treats them well. When I consult with clients, I encourage them to build their businesses by following my Ten Commandments of Business:

1. Respond to your customers' or clients' problems. Show them that their concerns are important to you by getting back to them quickly.
2. Solve your customers' or clients' problems. Find what they need and provide it.
3. Deliver what you promised or more. Underpromise and overdeliver.
4. Provide nothing less than top quality for the price. Provide the best value you can.
5. Charge a fair amount for your goods or services. Never gouge or overcharge.
6. Always deliver on time. If you can't, let the client know as soon as possible.

7. Be pleasant, polite, and responsive. Answer every question and call as soon as possible.
8. Respect others and their property. Never leave a mess.
9. After delivery, stand behind your goods and services. Check that customers and clients are satisfied and that what you have provided is working well. If not, fix it quickly without a fuss.
10. Satisfy your customers' by doing whatever it takes. Go the extra mile to agree on a satisfactory resolution.

If you follow these commandments, your business will set a standard for excellence that your customers and clients will love. When you establish a track record of excellence, your customers and clients will tell the world. They will extol your virtues and drum up new business for you.

Then, when you promote your business, your customers and clients will stand behind you. They will endorse you and refer new business to you. They will become your extended sales force.

When you follow my Ten Commandments of Business, your integrity, reliability, and record will speak for you. You will not be bragging; you will just be stating the facts.

■ ■ ■ **CONNECTING LINK** ■ ■ ■

When customers are pleased with your goods or services and believe that you provide good value, they won't shop around. They will keep doing business with you as long as the quality and value you provide do not drop. Retaining existing customers is essential for the bottom line because it costs five times more to get new customers than to retain existing clients.

■ ■ ■ ■ Acting Pleasantly

On the flip side, the best way to get great service is by being a great customer or client. If you treat people well, they will be more likely to extend themselves for you. If you're rude, brusque, or impolite, don't expect them to go out of their way for you.

Being an outstanding customer or client will help you get what you want and more. Providers will make greater efforts to keep you happy. Being a great customer or client also can increase your chances of getting referrals from the businesses that serve you.

Whenever you deal with service providers, do the following:

1. *Be pleasant, kind, and polite.* Courtesy and kindness are contagious. When you treat people kindly, most will reciprocate. Some will go out of their way to help you. Preface your requests with "please" and take a gentle, not demanding, tone. Don't be demeaning or show your impatience regardless of how frustrated you feel. It takes only a little effort to be pleasant, kind, and polite, but it can pay huge dividends.

2. *Smile.* Smiling cuts tension, conveys warmth, and can be disarming. A single smile can change the mood; it can break the gloom and turn a bad day great. When you smile, most people loosen up and find it harder to treat you harshly or meanly.

3. *Be understanding.* Service providers may want to help you but may be prevented by certain restrictions or rules. Try viewing the situation from their perspective and sympathize. When they see that you are making an effort to understand, they may be more likely to try to find ways to help you. For example, they may have some leeway, know how to bypass the rules, or know of exceptions.

4. *Offer viable alternatives.* When the usual approaches don't work, look for other options. Ask if other alternatives exist. Suggest other approaches, but when you do, offer them in the form of questions. For instance, ask, "What if you tried _____?" You may come up with an idea that the service provider never considered before.

5. *Clearly state your appreciation.* Thank people for their efforts—and mean it! Acknowledge that they did

something special. Don't gush or lay it on thickly, but leave no doubt that you are grateful for the efforts they made on your behalf.

▪ ▪ ▪ Responding

When customers or clients contact you with problems or questions, respond promptly. Have procedures in place to listen and, when necessary, to act, even if it's just to find out or clarify what they want. Many companies don't bother to respond, which often inflames the situation and makes it worse.

Respond quickly. Prompt responses can diffuse problems because they convey the message that you're concerned. When you respond rapidly, you may not have to do as much to satisfy the customer. If, however, customers are forced to wait, they will feel that you don't really care, and that will increase their anger.

"Actually read and consider their requests," Craig Newmark says. "Many companies don't." Make it clear that you are interested in their concerns even if it's just to clarify or find out precisely what they want.

Customer comments, questions, and complaints can be a terrific source of feedback. When your clients know that they have easy access to you, they can provide valuable insights and information. In addition, being accessible and responsive will improve your customer relations and boost your brand.

Some customers are unreasonable. However, as Newmark points out, "Some unreasonable customers can be reasoned with if you show them that you're honestly listening. However, there will be cases where you have to give up. Sometimes, no response is the proper response, and other times, you let them know patiently why it's difficult to work with them. Be compassionate, but tell them what the deal is," he adds.

It often pays to resolve problems quickly and get them out of the way, although that may be a bitter pill to swallow. At first, you may resent having to pay or accommodate customers, but it's usually worth the price in order to move on. In fact, over time, the amount you pay may turn out to be a bargain.

■ ■ ■ Heart-Centered Marketing

I believe in doing business from the heart by adopting a service mind-set, and actively looking for concrete ways to help. Helping is fulfilling and enables you to forge close bonds. Also, your help may be returned. More important, your focus on helping will put you in the vanguard of a new business revolution: heart-centered marketing.

Heart-centered marketing revolves around how you can help others instead of concentrating on how you can fill your own needs. Heart-centered marketers also look for opportunities to help others by identifying what they need and helping them get it. Heart-centered marketers constantly, not occasionally, ask how they can help others not as an expected part of their product or service but as a voluntary extra.

More people are practicing heart-centered marketing and proving that it is a powerful, viable, and fulfilling way to conduct business. The strength of heart-centered marketing is that helps people build closer relationships with like-minded people who share their values. I think it's the wave of the future.

Learn how you can help others by asking them the following questions directly:

- What goods or services do you need to increase your business? If your goods or services are not what they need, ask yourself if there is anyone you know who could fill their needs.
- Who could help you get to the next level? Determine what people you could connect them with who could support and make a difference to them.

When you answer both questions, act. Deliver goods or services that they can use or connect them with others who can.

In recent years, many major international product companies have adopted a service mind set. They have stopped simply being product companies and reinvented themselves as service providers that are in the solution business. Here's how they work.

Instead of trying to sell prospective customers their goods, they first identify their customers' problems and needs. Then they find ways to solve and satisfy them. They customize products and work with other companies to solve their customers' problems. Their objective is to build strong and close long-term relationships with their customers so that their customers will come to them to solve their future problems and needs. They are no longer simply interested in closing one-time sales.

Adopt this service mind set with your customers. Become their partners in solving their problems.

▪ ▪ ▪ Encouraging

Many people never receive encouragement. If you can support their efforts, even in small ways, it can help them dramatically. Frequently, just being there, listening, and uttering a few encouraging words can spur them on.

Brenda stopped me in the hall after I spoke at a conference in Dallas. She was extremely concerned about her business and asked me a few questions. I told her my thoughts, we chatted briefly, and I tried to encourage her.

About three months later Brenda called me. She told how helpful my encouragement had been and said that her business was thriving. Our conversation got her over a major obstacle, totally changing her perspective and her life. She emphasized how grateful she was.

I don't remember the questions Brenda asked me in Dallas, nor do I remember what I said. But her phone call reminded me how meaningful encouragement and words of kindness can be.

The fact that people stop, listen, and care can spur you on, help you turn the tide and succeed. When they understand, it makes you feel that you're not alone; it encourages you to continue. Hope is an unparalleled motivator; it can help us scale the highest, most daunting heights. Lack of hope is the opposite and can stop you dead in your tracks. Encouragement provides hope. When you encourage people, many of them will be grateful and look for opportunities to reciprocate, especially when your encouragement helped them succeed.

My client Lorrie Sullenberger developed a television show and worked for years to sell it to a network. One day she called me in extreme distress and told me how frustrated and discouraged she was. The constant negotiations, continual changes, and endless delays had taken their toll. She wanted to walk away, scrap it, give it all up, and take some mindless job.

I let her speak. I listened, sympathized, and was understanding. I really felt for her. When I thought that she had expressed herself fully, I encouraged her. I pointed out that she had a fabulous idea that would make a great show, she had done wonderful work, and a deal could be right around the corner, as indeed it was. Less than two weeks later she called to tell me the good news: A cable channel had made an offer, and she wanted to thank me for my encouragement.

■ ■ ■ **CONNECTING LINK** ■ ■ ■

Right before the finish line we can become exhausted. In the homestretch, the pain, pressure, and fear can hit their peak. At that time, we've put in so much time, effort, and work that the stakes are stratospheric and we desperately don't want to lose. It's easy to be discouraged and tempting to throw in the towel. That's why encouragement is so vital: It can be that little nudge that helps you reach your goals.

Frequently, people need to talk or complain. Just expressing themselves can defuse the intensity of their feelings and remove the sting. As they speak, you can see them calm down and become more at ease. Suddenly, solutions may become clearer to them. When they are more relaxed, they can approach their problems with less emotion, which can give them the clarity to work out their problems.

Blaming

When problems arise, don't cast blame. Finding fault with others doesn't solve problems; it can magnify them. Accusations serve to alienate others. Making accusations can damage your credibility and make your working relationships more difficult. When you blame others, your customers and clients may interpret it as making excuses that they don't want to hear regardless of how valid they may be. They only want results.

Even if you have decided never to work with a person again, don't accuse that person. It will get you nowhere. Accusations rarely solve problems, and they can get everyone upset. They can feed and intensify the flames.

Instead of blaming, broker solutions. Find common ground where all the parties can meet and help the project reach its goal. Suggest solutions that will make everyone as happy as possible under the circumstances, something they all can live with. Start the ball rolling by giving something; it will set the tone for a productive give-and-take.

When you know problems are looming and you won't be able to deliver as promised, tell your clients. When you are absolutely sure, let them know so that they can make all the necessary adjustments and prepare for the delay. Try to estimate when the problem will be resolved and then work like mad to deliver on or before that date.

If others know that you are always trying to solve problems and deliver as promised, they will be more likely to continue working with you and recommend you to others.

Action Plan

1. What are the Ten Commandments of Business?

_____

_____

_____

_____

_____

_____

_____

_____

_____

_____

2. Hope can you improve the service you get from service providers?

_____

_____

_____

3. What questions should you ask to discover people's needs?

_____

_____

_____

4. Describe how heart-centered marketing could work for you.

_____

_____

_____

_____

■ ■ ■ ■ ■ ■ ■ ■ ■ ■ ■ ■ ■ ■ ■ ■ ■ ■

15

Be Flexible and Keep Your Options Open

This chapter covers:

- Control
- Emergencies
- Rules
- Mistakes

ACCORDING TO ANTHROPOLOGISTS, we human beings have survived as a species because of our adaptability. Other creatures became extinct when they could not adjust to changing conditions, but we managed to endure because we developed the ability to change and adapt.

That asset—the ability to adjust—is also essential in business because so much can change. Nothing in business is etched in stone. Appointments, meetings, and projects are canceled routinely. Major deals go down the drain. People you work with take other jobs. Orders are revised, and people and goods are delayed or never show up. Natural disasters occur, wars break out, and labor unions strike. New technology makes your forte obsolete.

In today's business climate, customers and clients want to limit their risks. When they do business with you or recommend you, they want to know that you will perform well regardless of the surprises that occur. You must show that you're flexible, that you can adapt to the unexpected challenges that always seem to arise and make the best of them.

Today, being the top expert in your field and having unparalleled experience may not be enough. Since business is now so susceptible to change, you cannot sit still. Instead, you must look ahead, anticipate problems that could arise, and develop the flexibility to handle them. You also must project how your business will develop, where it will be tomorrow, and what other opportunities might arise.

"When you're looking at growing and scaling a business, you must be flexible," Sandra Yancey advises. "There is a difference between seizing a transformational opportunity and being distracted, and sometimes the distinction is gray. Starbucks has a history of looking for transformational opportunities: Moving into music, bottled drinks, and ice cream seemed to work, but publishing a magazine didn't."

"It can be a problem," Yancey notes. "If you're too myopic, you can miss opportunities, but if you extend too far, you could reach beyond the expertise and qualities that brought you success. At eWomenNetwork we have tried to focus on who is our core customer and what are we trying to serve. Since our core customers are women and we are trying to serve all the marketing needs they have to build their businesses, we created four major divisions that promote women and their businesses." Those divisions give eWomenNetwork the flexibility to help its members handle a wide range of problems. Also, the members know that they can do business with, recommend, and rely on other eWomenNetwork members.

Control

When problems arise and surprises occur, they throw projects off course. Distinguish yourself by limiting the damage they create by having a flexible mind set. Examine your operation, review your procedures, and think of various options. Incorporate that mind set into your business; make it part of the culture.

Most things don't go according to a script. You frequently have to ad-lib. Being spontaneous, addressing changes, and even reversing your field can be exciting, creative, and productive. It can sharpen your skills and your mind. Your ability to change and adapt will be noticed and admired.

You can't anticipate every problem; you can't always be in control. Problems will arise that you can't predict or prevent. Something will alter your plans. If you try to anticipate every possible calamity, it will drive you crazy and provide no guarantees.

Instead, expect the unexpected. Understand that change is inevitable and don't worry so much about what form that change will take. Proceed with your plans, continue to conduct your business vigorously, and don't let up.

Make flexibility part of your company's culture by teaching your staff to expect change. When they plan, instruct them to think of other options, paths that they could take if changes occur. Just identifying possible alternatives will help your people develop flexible mind sets. Then, when problems arise—as they will—your organization will be poised to respond more capably.

If you and your staff think in terms of being flexible, unexpected changes won't be as devastating and you will be able to respond quickly and effectively. You may even be able to turn them to your advantage.

Emergencies

Clients often call me when they need immediate help. They have called me when I'm in transit, on vacation, or trying to relax at home. Usually, an emergency arose and they need to know, "What should I do? What should I say? How should I act?"

Needless to say, these calls can be disruptive because they tend to come at the worst possible times. Regardless of how busy I am and how inconvenient the calls are, I try to respond immediately or as soon as possible. I try to be flexible, alter my schedule, and help.

On occasion, it's impossible for me to talk, and so I call my distressed clients and say, "Look, I can't talk to you right now, but I'll call you as soon as I can." If the problem seems major or if the client is extremely upset, I ask a few questions to understand the problem and tell the client what to do before we speak again. Then I make sure to call back the first chance I get.

Clients who call for help with emergencies frequently cannot think clearly. Something has frightened them and locked their minds. In these situations, here's how I proceed:

- I stress that they should take their time and tell me everything. Usually, just knowing that they have my time and attention quickly helps them focus, organize their thoughts, and be more at ease.
- I remain calm. I know my clients are upset, and my composure steadies them. As they settle down, they tend to express themselves more clearly.
- I let them speak as long as they want and listen closely to make sure that I understand the problem and exactly what they fear. As they speak, they often realize what they should do, and the intensity of their emotions abates.
- I restate the problem and lay out their fears to let them know that I understand them and make sure that we are on the same wavelength.
- I address my clients' problems and tell them how I think they should proceed.
- We discuss my plan, and I answer their questions.
- When we agree on how they will proceed, I ask them to repeat exactly what they are going to do.

Frequently, panicky clients just need a little hand-holding and support. Listen to their questions because hearing them out can be helpful. Walk them through the problem, explore the best solutions, and work together to create plans for implementing solutions.

When you help clients with emergencies, they never seem to forget. They repeatedly express their appreciation and emphasize how important it was that you were there during their time of need. It's what they remember and frequently appreciate the most. Plus, it can make you feel great!

■ ■ ■ **CONNECTING LINK** ■ ■ ■

When disasters and emergencies strike, deal with them even if they are mostly in your clients' minds. Give them your time and attention. Put out all raging fires before their world burns down. Attend to the major problem and get it under control. When your clients and customers need you, be there for them.

Certain clients and customers are always panic-stricken; these high-maintenance, overly dramatic individuals constantly demand your attention. Usually they sap your energy and wear you out. These clients are not worth the aggravation they cause and are rarely good referral sources. Get them out of your life!

■ ■ ■ Rules

In business, you must have rules. You cannot operate a successful business without structure and procedures or it will be chaotic. Rules provide stability for you, your employees, and your customers. When everyone knows the rules, fewer disputes occur.

Rules also encourage commitment from your clients and customers. If they don't commit or make enough of an investment, they may be more likely to cancel, not give their all, or not follow through. If they don't succeed, they may blame you.

In practice, rules work about 80 percent of the time. In the remaining 20 percent of cases, be flexible. Operate on the basis of reason. Understand the underlying reason for each of your rules: why it exists, the purpose it was intended to serve. Then, when incidents occur, identify the rule involved, examine its purpose, and decide how it should be applied.

For the courses I teach, I have a no-refund policy. When I offer a course, a number of considerations come into play. I must attract a minimum number of attendees for my programs to be financially viable. If fewer people attend, the fees I receive may not cover my expenses. When more people enroll, I may need to get a larger space, rent more equipment, or provide more materials. I also may need additional help. To make these decisions and create the ideal course environment, I need to know how many people will attend each of my programs in advance. Therefore, when someone cancels or misses a sessions, I do not issue a refund.

However, if a person enrolls in one of my programs and an emergency occurs, I am flexible and refund the fee. In each situation, I try to be reasonable, understanding, and humane.

Whenever I make decisions, I try to be kind, compassionate, and understanding. I reverse positions and ask how I would want to be treated if I were the other person. I've adopted this stance because I know how much I have appreciated it when people were kind to me and gave me breaks, and so I try to pass their kindness on to others.

■ ■ ■ **CONNECTING LINK** ■ ■ ■

In addition to my business acumen, I want to be noticed for my kindness and compassion. When people talk about me, I hope those qualities are stressed. That's what I would like in my life.

However, if you need reasons other than being kind and understanding or doing the right thing, try this: People remember your good deeds and may reward you for them. They may come back and give you more business, praise you, or recommend others to you.

Life is complex. People have too much on their plates. They are so overcommitted that they don't have enough time, and that puts them under enormous stress. You may have to break or relax your rules to get their full attention. If you doggedly enforce the rules, some people will be resentful. They may feel that you're not understanding or kind enough to work with. And they will express their feelings to others.

People need some slack; after all, they are not machines. If someone is usually prompt and reliable, give him or her a break if he or she is late or misses one time. Don't dole out punishment.

I like to say, "Life happens." Everything doesn't fit neatly into the rules or always go on schedule. Let your business reflect life. Be supportive of the people who give you business. If they need a break or a change, give it to them.

■ ■ ■ Mistakes

People make mistakes. Often the mistakes are unintentional, but they still cause harm. Be understanding and forgiving, not harsh. Most people know when they mess up and feel bad about it; they don't have to be told or reminded. Assume that they got the message. Most will appreciate the fact that you didn't lecture them or make them feel worse.

When you act kindly and with understanding, the recipients of your largesse will be grateful. Your understanding could help you make a friend, follower, or supporter who could send business to you. It's a great way to build a corps of loyal followers. However, if you treat those who make mistakes harshly, they will avoid you and tell others how badly you treated them. They certainly won't do business with you or refer others to you.

Don't be afraid to make mistakes, especially when it comes to people. Give them the benefit of the doubt; don't suspect their motives. If you try to be understanding, people will respond and work to live up to your expectations, and that can pay dividends.

If you make mistakes, learn from them; try not to repeat those mistakes. Don't punish yourself. Take the same approach you use with others—forgive.

Action Plan

1. What steps can you take to establish a culture of flexibility in your business?

_____

_____

_____

_____

2. How would you deal with a client who makes a panic-stricken emergency telephone call?

_____

_____

_____

_____

3. What does the underlying basis for your rules mean, and why is it important?

_____

_____

_____

_____

4. Give three examples of times when you could have been more flexible with your clients or customers.

_____

_____

_____

_____

16

Fill It With Magic

This chapter covers:

- It's up to you
- Creating magic
- Adjust, alter, combine
- Dr. Proactive
- Take the initiative
- Barter and exchange

NOW THAT YOU KNOW how be noticed, take an additional step: Make what you're doing bigger and more memorable. Move it up a notch, add pizzazz, and make it sing. Surprise people with the unexpected; make them sit up and be amazed. Be unique, brighten the colors, choose a new palette, and toss in extra spice. Take chances and keep topping yourself. Spread change and excitement throughout your world in big, bold colorful strokes. Turn on the magic.

As I stated at the beginning of this book, getting noticed to grow your business is a continual process that takes a lot of work. For the most part, you must concentrate on a ton of details that may not be very exciting or glamorous. In fact, when you are putting it all together, it may be pretty dull. That's the time to strike. Find ways to liven it up, add a spark, and inject new life. Find the little twist that could shake things up.

Magic comes in many forms, and we all have it within us. It's just a matter of trying new and different ingredients in your recipe. Experiment, take chances, and break the mold; try to connect with your magic. Keep trying because your magic may be deeply hidden, but believe me, it's there.

My magic is in connecting and seeing possibilities. I can build relationships with other people, see their potential, and find ways in which my contacts or I can work with them. My magic can help make others stars. Your magic could be writing, selling, decorating, making wine, or restoring vintage cars. It could be your insights, thoroughness, organization, judgment, or imagination. It could be your good looks or your wealth.

Find your magic and put on a show, a spectacular. Don't just do a job; put on a star-spangled extravaganza—soar. Go the extra 10 miles.

■ ■ ■   CONNECTING LINK   ■ ■ ■

Magic begets magic; it initiates a chain of magical reactions and events. When you create magic, the benefits you receive also can be magical. Those benefits can be experiential; they can give you great enjoyment and stimulation and help you learn, branch out, and grow. They can energize your projects and advance the state of the art.

When you create magic, the benefits you reap can be leads or referrals, or involvement in interesting new subjects. Subsequently, someone could speak with you about those subjects. He or she might say, "Oh, I didn't realize that you knew so much about that subject. I know a person who could really use your help."

Don't settle for the ordinary; it will put you to sleep. Sure, you'll get the job done, but you will miss out on the excitement, fun, and growth. Invest in yourself. Push to surpass your previous best. Each advance will raise you to a new level and bring you closer to the stars.

▪ ▪ ▪ It's Up to You

By now you know what you do well and why others want to work with you. That's where your magic lies. Now apply it and let it work its wonders. Put the process in motion by exploring these areas:

- How you can improve your goods and services and deliver even more
- How you can enhance your talent and skill to deliver even more
- How you can make it more fun, more noteworthy, and more unusual

Think on a larger scale; go beyond the usual limits. Try to eliminate all unnecessary steps and simplify the process. Always try to give, produce, and satisfy more.

Brainstorm. Toss ideas around with your staff, consultants, advisors, and trusted friends. Be outlandish, stretch the limits, see what you come up with, and enjoy the process.

"Deliver what you deliver in a way that is unique, consistent with who you really are," Tommy Newberry, the author of *Success Is Not an Accident* (Tyndale House Publishers, 2007), suggests. "It will be more fun and you will perform better because you are being true to yourself; you will have something that stands out and that you won't have to fake. When you are true to yourself, your message will come through."

Create your own magic. Magicians don't pull rabbits out of hats the first time they try. They have to find out how the trick works, get all the necessary items, and then practice repeatedly until they can perform flawlessly every time. Practice and don't be afraid to stumble and fall. Get up and try again and again. Before long, you will master the art.

I find the synchronicity of meeting new people, connecting with them, and working with them magical. I love the way the process unfolds. I'm amazed by how well all the parts fit when you're both of one mind, totally excited, and can't wait to bring it to a higher level. That's when the creativity soars and the breakthroughs occur.

Watch out for repetition; repetition kills. Doing the same thing over and over will bore you to death eventually regardless of how successful you become. The difficult part is that it's often hard to change. Clients and customers want what you have done successfully before, their money and acclaim are hard to resist, and you're frequently pressed for time.

Serve your clients and yourself by always looking ahead, seeing what you could do differently and better. If you fall into a rut, you could lose your edge; competitors and upstarts could overtake you.

Experiment, explore. When you keep your mind engaged and challenged, magic can occur. Refreshing your approaches can add new energy all around. Your clients will love your new ideas; they will be excited by the directions you suggest. They will appreciate your efforts to constantly improve.

You also will share in the benefits because constant new input can be captivating. It can sweep you toward new vistas and discoveries that can make your work more stimulating, satisfying, and fun. It can enhance the quality of your work and the other aspects of your life.

■ ■ ■ Creating Magic

I believe in magic. In fact, I titled my last book *Networking Magic* because I am convinced that when certain events come together, a synergy occurs that takes things to another level. I find those experiences absolutely magical.

You can be plodding along when suddenly all the pieces fit together and fall into place. Problems seem to disappear or get solved, and you move smoothly ahead. Everyone wants to jump on the band-wagon and share in the fun; it's hugely exciting.

When the magic takes hold, you can feel it. It's like a switch has been thrown that makes everything sparkle. When it happens, you know that you are involved with something special, and so does everyone else.

I also believe that magic can be self-generating, that we can turn it on. You can create magic, but first you must put certain pieces into place. You must take the following steps:

- Know yourself: your strengths and weaknesses. To make a strong connection, you must be able to express clearly what you bring to the partnership: your talents and abilities. If you know your shortcomings, you understand the type of help you need and who to form liaisons with.

- Know what you want to create and accomplish: your short-term and long-term goals. Even an ideal blending of talent won't be productive for you if you and your partner's goals are opposed. You may want to build a solid long-term career, while your partner is interesting in making a big one-time score and getting out of the business.

- Be willing to ask others if they want to work with you or if they know others who would be a good match for you. If you expect others to approach you, prepare for a long wait. Don't expect magic to appear magically. Prime the pump and see what flows.

- Be open to possibilities. People may not want to go in the direction you have in mind. They often have their own agendas to pursue. The fact that they have clear ideas and objectives should not eliminate them as potential partners. If you are otherwise well matched, see how you could both fulfill your needs. Also, be open to venturing in new directions provided that they don't force you too far afield.

- Use all your senses. Examine matters with each of the five senses: sight, sound, smell, taste, and touch. Look at them one at a time, and when you have considered all five, try combining some of their features.

Look to nature. Frank Lloyd Wright was an inventive, iconoclastic architect whose work still awes people. Wright believed that to be creative, you must be in tune with nature. In fact, Wright spelled the word with a capital N. He didn't believe that you should copy nature but that you should see inside it and try to find something new.

Change your perspective. Instead of always looking straight on, stand to the side. Approach objects from the rear, from above, from underneath, and at angles. Distort or blur your focus, reverse colors, move the parts around, or let some borders float.

Turn to your fantasies and ask, "What if?" Banish logic and reason to the back of your mind. Develop ideas and objectives, deal in possibilities, and then explore ways to make them work.

Magic struck for Alex Mandosian on a warm fall evening in 2002 when he couldn't find a place to park at a shopping center. All the spaces were taken because Al and Tipper Gore were signing books at a bookshop in the center. "How pathetic that a former vice president of the United States has to spend so much time and effort to sell books," Mandosian thought. Then it stuck him that by using the telephone and the Internet he could produce virtual book tours that would not require authors to travel and would enable them to sell substantially more books.

Since then Mandosian has been running virtual book tours for numerous best-selling authors. The idea has caught on, and virtual book tours have become an integral part of book promotion. In fact, except for rare exceptions, virtual tours have replaced actual book tours for most publishing companies.

■ ■ ■ Adjust, Alter, Combine

To be creative and think out of the box, you don't have to invent or discover something completely new. You don't have to invent the lightbulb, but you can change it. You can make it brighter, longer-lasting, more energy-efficient, solar-powered, or recyclable.

Take chances, go against the grain, try something new. Go in new directions; combine items that already exist in ways that have not been tried before. Find how you could take what you're doing and make it new and different. Try turning it inside out, upside down, and on its side or even break it in two. See how you can make it more exciting and compelling and have more benefit to you, your clients, and your customers.

Playing it safe will provide some results, but to set yourself apart, you have to step out of your comfort zone and take risks. You have to keep pushing, moving forward, and thinking.

Owen Morse and Jon Wee of the comedy juggling team The Passing Zone wanted to create a piece for their show that involved juggling chain saws. Since other performers already had juggled chain saws, they wanted to come up with a routine that differed and made a big splash.

They took a chance. They decided to combine chain saws with ballet because "it would be an interesting juxtaposition from the roaring macho of chain saws to the delicacy of ballet," Morse recalls. They bought tights, hired a professional choreographer, and put it all together. The juggling chain saws routine has been a huge success and one of the signature pieces for which The Passing Zone has been acclaimed.

▥ ▥ ▥ Dr. Proactive

Dr. Proactive (Randy Gilbert) decided to build his network by starting Inside Success Radio, a series of Internet radio programs, and the results have been magical. His show has a strong following, has strengthened his network, and has created new lucrative business ventures for him.

On the Internet, radio shows are broadcast on an endless variety of subjects. Gilbert's concentrates on interviewing authors. The program has given Gilbert many benefits. It's enabled him to read loads of interesting books, talk about them with their authors, and create relationships with many of those authors.

Starting the program was inexpensive. Interviews are recorded by telephone without the use of special high-priced equipment. Software to record interviews on a computer can be obtained free of charge. Gilbert now offers a course, the Secrets of Internet Radio (www.secretsofinternetradio.com), that teaches people how to start, operate, and promote Internet radio programs.

Many authors have promoted their books on Inside Success Radio. "And once you promote them, they will go out of their way to promote you," Gilbert revealed. Many became Gilbert's joint venture partners and used their lists to help promote other authors' books.

"I instantly get past gatekeepers when I tell them I'm the producer of an Internet radio show," Gilbert revealed. "I'm immediately transferred to the person I want, and they're happy to talk. It opens doors everywhere, exactly like a press pass. I get into conventions, meetings, seminars, where I meet really interesting people."

"When people learn that I have a radio show, they share information with me that they haven't previously disclosed. When they know it's for the radio, they want to give something special."

■ ■ ■ Take the Initiative

When you create magic, don't just sit back and expect the magic to work by itself. Help it along. Magic usually doesn't occur in isolation; it tends to be a by-product of other actions; it must be generated.

Patti D. Hill of BlabberMouth Marketing & Public Relations related the following experience:

"We heard Goliath was looking for a partner to create a new branding campaign. We were up against some big dogs that were going to give us some pretty stiff competition. Having the name BlabberMouth doesn't hurt. We're expected to come up with cool ideas. We did. It was called 'Get Your Brand Smokin'.'"

"Our Get Your Brand Smokin' brochure is a little five- by seven-inch piece printed on smoky brown paper and tape-bound. We packaged it inside a stained cigar box with the BlabberMouth logo 'branded' on the lid. The brochure described the concept of branding in a step-by-step lesson, listed the ways BlabberMouth approaches the branding, and closed with an overview of our company and our competencies—short and succinct."

That was a good idea, but Hill says that for added magic, "we included a few cigars and a lighter in the box. A 'Blabber Girl' wearing cowboy boots and hat delivered the package. When a rep from the behemoth's marketing department received the package, you should have seen her jaw drop! We hammered them!"

"We received telephone calls from the prospect's marketing manager and so impressed the team that several employees want to come and work for us. They want to be where magic was made."

Look for opportunities to trigger the magic, situations in which you could create more. When you find them, help the magic take hold by vigorously pursuing each opportunity. Create the right conditions by following these steps:

1. Examine each project and each of its components. Before you begin a project, see what you could add to improve it and make it shine. As you work on a venture, ask how you could make each step more special and exciting.
2. Get input from others. Ask your customers, clients, and vendors, along with the people with whom you work, how you could take projects to the next level. Solicit their opinions and insights. Contact experts and authorities to learn how you could add extra twists that could make your goods and services more magical, more distinct.
3. Continue working aggressively on your projects; pursue your agendas and see them through. Don't go off dreaming and allow them to fall apart. Clearly tell everyone involved what you need and precisely how he or she can help.

Look for inspiration. Take a page from the most exciting people, the empire builders who work on a huge scale: Bill Gates, Oprah Winfrey, Donald Trump, Madonna, Richard Branson, Rupert Murdoch, and Steve Jobs. Study them and other magicians, especially those in your field:

- Examine what they created.
- Understand why it's so great.
- Learn what they did differently.
- Identify the boundaries they pushed.
- Analyze their methods and procedures.
- Find out how they broke the mold.

Determine what you can borrow from them and incorporate in your business. Think about it and make it happen.

Mail Messages

Add magic by adding pizzazz to your voice mail message. "Your voice mail is an underutilized yet incredibly important tool," Branding Specialist David Tyreman, the author of *World Famous* (AMACOM, 2008) reminds us. "Use your outgoing message to position yourself, to set yourself up as an authority, as an expert, as the most important person on the planet to solve callers' problems. If your message says something like "I'm either on the on the phone or away from my desk," its boring and should be replaced.

Give the first words you say the highest value, Tyreman suggests, so they create a strong immediate impression for you. Don't waste the prime opportunity by being dull. Instead, engage and inspire. "Be creative, brainstorm, decide what you want callers to get from your message and how do you want them to feel when they hear it. If your outgoing message doesn't make callers respond with comments such as, 'Wow, great message," re-record it.

Tyreman says your message should not exceed 15 seconds, should leave callers wanting more, and make the callers more eager and excited to do business with you. "I've been hired for $100,000.00 contracts on the strength of my voice mail message so don't let your insecurity or discomfort stop you from expressing yourself; there's big money on the line when you choose to get noticed," Tyreman declares.

■ ■ ■ Barter and Exchange

I find that exchanging or bartering goods and services can be magical, remarkably productive, and a wonderful way to get noticed. When people know that you are willing to swap goods and services, many of them will be more willing to do business with you.

I've frequently bartered. I've written press releases, consulted, and provided other services in exchange for products and services. Many of those with whom I have swapped have become my clients, and I received another benefit: Since I used their goods and services, I became personally familiar with them. Now I know their strong points, how well they work; I can smell them, taste them, and feel their texture. My experience helps me describe their benefits more clearly, accurately, and passionately, which helps me promote them more effectively.

Bartering has helped me build closer, more personal client relationships. I think these bonds stem from the fact that I actually use their goods and services and feel that I have more of a personal stake in their success.

Bartering is an excellent way to build new businesses. It helps people who may be short on funds but need your goods or services. Frequently, the fact that they don't have to lay out cash is important to them. It can be the clincher that convinces them to hire you.

When you barter, you can get in on the ground floor with your clients. You can learn about their businesses, values, and objectives.

You can become an asset to them, solve problems for them, and grow with them as they build their businesses.

Exchanging goods and services has a helping, personal, and humane aspect that makes me feel good. I've found that when people who barter are pleased with the results they receive, they frequently throw in a little extra to say thanks. I treasure those little gifts and appreciate the gestures.

Bartering can take many forms. It can be on a purely professional and service-oriented level. A colleague asked me if I would e-mail an announcement of the publication of her upcoming book to the people on my list. I agreed to do it, and we discussed the announcement and what it should contain. I made a number of suggestions that I thought would intrigue the people on my list, and we ended up writing a terrific announcement together.

When we completed the announcement, I made one request. I told her that I was writing *Get Noticed . . . Get Referrals* and asked if she would e-mail an announcement to those on her list before its release. She quickly agreed, and we started brainstorming about my announcement. As we bounced ideas around, the magic kicked in. We began laughing, got very creative, and came up with an inspired plan. The process was so enjoyable and so productive that we made plans to collaborate again.

Bartering can take place on a large scale. Jay Conrad Levinson has been treated to VIP trips all over the world in exchange for his writing and speaking services. I've been given luxury cruises to exotic locales for making shipboard speeches and presentations.

"Today, more businesses are open to bartering, so for most people it makes great sense," Levinson states. "It's usually cost-effective for companies to give you their products in exchange for your services. I've bartered for big-ticket items, including trips, cruises, giant-screen TVs, and a solar heating system for my home and pool. And in all cases, I've had a great experience and received top-of-the-line goods and services."

In addition to hiring me for my public relations services, clients employ me for my contacts and connections, which can save them time, energy, and money. Everyone has contacts that he or she can use to help others. Most people have insights and know shortcuts that others could use, but they rarely focus on them.

Think of your contacts and connections as items that you could exchange or barter. Identify those which could be helpful and who they could aid. Then explore what you could receive in exchange. Your contacts and connections could be a major unused asset for you.

Action Plan

1. Identify the benefits you could derive by putting more magic in your work.

_____

_____

_____

_____

2. What three actions could you take to create more magic in your work?

_____

_____

_____

_____

3. What advantages could you get by bartering?

_____

_____

_____

_____

4. What specific steps could you take to add magic to one of your current projects?

_____

_____

_____

_____

_____

17

Summing Up

THANK YOU FOR READING this book. I hope that you found it helpful and productive.

In these pages I've told you about many ways to get noticed and grow your business, and I would like to leave you with some final thoughts that I hope will remain with you. Although I've mentioned most of them already, I feel that they are so important that they bear repeating. I believe they are vital in getting noticed and living a fulfilling life. Here they are:

- Be yourself. Build on your assets and your uniqueness because they are what people want. Clients and customers want you, your special viewpoint or approach, your unique insights or touch, not a weak imitation of someone else. Don't just be a copycat; find your own voice. Get noticed in your own way, in the manner most natural and comfortable to you. Examine the approaches that others have taken and then do what feels natural for you. Trust yourself and your instincts.

- Work your business around your life so that it fits into your life, supports your life, and reflects you. Too many people do the reverse: They work their lives around their businesses, and it frequently doesn't work out well.
- Think of your clients, customers, referral sources, vendors, and suppliers as your partners and friends, as people who want to help you. Never forget that they're people, not just business statistics, and that you cannot succeed without them.
- Master the art of listening because when you listen, you truly learn. If you listen, people will want to share their knowledge with you, be with you, and help you. They will consider you their friend and go to great lengths to help you.
- Before you take on any project, make sure that you know exactly what the client or customer wants. Put your understanding in writing to eliminate doubt. It's hard to satisfy people when you don't know what they want.
- Be generous. Make giving a central part of your life. Work hard and give your clients and customers more than they expect. Give people your time. Always show your appreciation by thanking and rewarding those who help you. Praise others and give them the credit and the spotlight.
- Surround yourself with the most interesting, active, and positive people. Hang around with experts, authorities, and people who are smarter and more accomplished than you. Find ways to meet them and be with them because they will open amazing new doors for you. They will support your efforts, make them stronger, and add fullness and excitement to your life.
- Constantly strive for excellence; try to do everything in the best possible way. Build a reputation for continually doing outstanding work, and everyone will want to be with and work with you. People who live out their excellence will find you.

- Always ask, can I do it better, more interestingly, or more inventively? Challenge yourself to go beyond your prior accomplishments and to always surpass your best. Constantly look in new directions.
- Never compromise your integrity. Stand by your values but don't preach. Always be truthful, honest, fair, understanding, and humane. Deliver what you promised when you promised.

Follow these suggestions and you will be noticed. The best people will notice and appreciate you. And you will enjoy a wonderful life!

Index

About the Author

Jill Lublin is an acclaimed international speaker who teaches powerful, innovative techniques on how to be influential, network, and build thriving businesses. The coauthor of two bestselling books, *Guerrilla Publicity* (Adams Media Corp., 2002) and *Networking Magic* (Adams Media Corp., 2004), she is also the founder of GoodNews Media, Inc., the host of a TV program, *The Connecting Minute*, and the nationally syndicated radio show *Do the Dream*.

As a media expert, Jill knows what the media wants and specializes in breaking down complex ideas in ways that are easy to follow, understand, and achieve. As the CEO of the strategic consulting firm Promising Promotion, Jill has shown numerous companies and individuals how to boost their bottom lines. In the past 20 years, she has worked with ABC, NBC, CBS, and other national media. The clients Jill has helped include banks, software and product companies, international conferences, speakers, nonprofit organizations, entertainment professionals, authors, and business operators of all sizes.

Jill has been featured in *The New York Times, Women's Day, Fortune Small Business, Inc*, and *Entrepreneur Magazine*, and on ABC and NBC radio and TV national affiliates. Her riveting and inspiring presentations to national associations, CEOs, and a wide range of business professionals have received rave reviews.

Get $50,000 Worth of Free Publicity

Are you a businessperson who is looking for . . .

- **MORE CLARITY?**
- **MORE VISIBILITY?**
- **MORE PROFITABILITY?**
- **MORE CREDIBILITY?**
- **MORE MARKET SHARE?**
- **CUTTING ADVERTISING COSTS IN HALF?**

This five-month program is for companies and individual businesses who want increased profits with less costs through media exposure. These five months will give you 10 individualized and focused coaching sessions and a monthly mastermind teleseminar addressing the following areas:

- Specific coaching custom-designed for you that will take you on your step-by-step PR journey and get the results you desire and deserve
- Mastering your message
- Defining your problem/solution
- Presenting your business/talent in powerful ways
- Reviewing your program and retrieving the dollars you are throwing away right now
- Defining your audiences and finding your niche
- Expanding and developing creative and unique ways to reach new audiences
- Creating a bio that positions you as the expert in your field
- Creating an announcement
- Writing a powerful press release
- Zooming in on a media list
- Scripting media—follow-up for you or your support team
- Media training for you or your staff member to make you sound like a star
- Enabling you to look yourself in the mirror and confidently claim yourself as an expert
- Establishing a monthly mastermind circle for *only* your inside-circle clients
- Learning the secrets that PR agencies charge you THOUSANDS of dollars per month for and actually being able to accomplish them at less than a third of the cost and in a five-month time frame unheard of in the PR world!

This five-month program is set up to identify and highlight some of your key needs, both general and specific. Included in our work together is the creation of one key press release. During this time, we will identify and provide several tangible, cost-effective public relations solutions you can access and implement immediately.

For more information about this program, go to our Web site, www.JillLublin.com; e-mail us at info@JillLublin.com; or phone (415) 883–5455.

• • •

Read what some of Jill's clients have to say about Jill's programs:

"I am thrilled to share that before the end of the program, one of Jill's ideas created over $100,000 in revenues for my business! Her coaching was effective, strategic and right on the money!"

—**Charlotte MacIlraith,** Ceramic Tile Refinishers

"Jill Lublin is the gold standard when it comes to understanding the true nature of publicity and how to get the most of it while getting the most from it."

—**Jay Conrad Levinson,** author of the bestselling series *Guerrilla Marketing*

"Jill is masterful at getting to the heart of the story. She thinks in headlines and sound bytes. In her dynamic and encouraging style, she brilliantly coached us to forget the subplots and hone in on the key points of the message."

—**Anita Halton,** Anita Halton Associates

"Working with Jill is like having a major NYC marketing agency share their best ideas at a fraction of the cost. She is brilliant!"

—**Pat Burns,** Millionaire Summit, General Manager

To download a free audio program with Jill and other experts on how to Get Noticed . . . Get Referrals and Be Influential, visit: http://www.getnoticedgetreferrals.com/bonus/

CPSIA information can be obtained
at www.ICGtesting.com
Printed in the USA
BVOW03s0303150217

476207BV00014B/137/P